Southern Literary Studies

Fred Hobson, Editor

Talking About William Faulkner

TALKING ABOUT WILLIAM FAULKNER

Interviews with Jimmy Faulkner and Others

SALLY WOLFF WITH FLOYD C. WATKINS

LOUISIANA STATE UNIVERSITY PRESS
Baton Rouge and London

Copyright © 1996 by Louisiana State University Press
All rights reserved
Manufactured in the United States of America
First printing
05   04   03   02   01   00   99   98   97   96   5   4   3   2   1

Designer: Amanda McDonald Key
Typeface: Sabon
Typesetter: Impressions Book and Journal Services, Inc.
Printer and binder: Thomson-Shore, Inc.

Library of Congress Cataloging-in-Publication Data

Faulkner, Jim, 1923–
    Talking about William Faulkner : interviews with Jimmy Faulkner,
and others / Sally Wolff with Floyd C. Watkins.
        p.   cm.   (Southern literary studies)
    Includes bibliographical references (p.   ) and index.
    ISBN 0-8071-2030-8 (cl : alk. paper)
    1. Faulkner, William, 1897–1962—Homes and haunts—Mississippi—
Lafayette County.   2. Faulkner, William, 1897–1962—Homes and
haunts—Mississippi—Oxford.   3. Novelists, American—20th century—
Family relationships.   4. Literary landmarks—Mississippi—
Lafayette County.   5. Literary landmarks—Mississippi—Oxford.
6. Faulkner, William, 1897–1962—Family.   7. Lafayette County
(Miss.)—Biography.   8. Faulkner, Jim, 1923-   —Interviews.
9. Oxford (Miss.)—Biography.   10. Faulkner family.   I. Wolff,
Sally.   II. Watkins, Floyd C.   III. Title.   IV. Series.
PS3511.A86Z78285   1996
813'.52—dc20
[B]   95-39359
                                                           CIP

Portions of Chapter 5 were first published as "Brother Will's Passing," *Southern Living* (March, 1992),
108–109, and are reprinted with permission.

For my parents,
Haskell and Elaine Wolff,
with love

Jim is the only person who likes me for what I am.

—William Faulkner

CONTENTS

ILLUSTRATIONS

ACKNOWLEDGMENTS

Research for this book was supported in part by a grant from the Emory University Research Committee. These interviews are taken from tapes in the Floyd C. Watkins Collection, Special Collections Department, Robert W. Woodruff Library, Emory University, Atlanta, Georgia. Annual trips to Lafayette County received the financial assistance of the Dean of Emory College and the Chair of the Department of English. We are deeply appreciative of David Minter for his support of the project and his excellent suggestions and revisions. Thanks to Jimmy Faulkner, Pearle Galloway, and Motee Daniel for permission to publish their interviews; to Mrs. Anna Webb, wife of the former curator of Rowan Oak, the late Dr. James Webb, for permission to publish the interview with Dr. Webb; to Howard Bahr, former curator of Rowan Oak (1984–1993), for his guidance, information about the history of Rowan Oak, suggestions, and other materials; and to Cynthia Shearer, present curator of Rowan Oak, for her support of the project and assistance with class tours. Special thanks to Eric and Marie Nitschke and Gretta Boers of the Woodruff Library Reference Department for their extraordinary skill and expertise in locating obscure documents. We are grateful to our research assistants, Joseph McElrath and Geoffrey Sive, for their dedication to the tasks of research, footnotes, and manuscript typing and revising, and to Samuel Wolff, Marcia Cranberg, and Conrad DeBold we express our appreciation for editorial assistance. Thanks to the many secretarial staff members who have assisted over the years in the transcription of the tape recordings, typing, and computerizing.

Our deep appreciation to Anna Watkins and Frederick King for their support and patience in listening to so much discourse about Faulkner.

Photographs are by Billy Howard except where noted.

ABOUT JIMMY FAULKNER,
PEARLE GALLOWAY, AND MOTEE DANIEL

Oxford, Mississippi, has long been home for Jimmy Faulkner, just as it was for his father, John, and uncle William Faulkner. Jimmy was born at home on University Avenue, July 18, 1923. He attended high school not only in Oxford but also in Greenville, Greenwood, and Clarksdale, Mississippi, and Whitehaven, Tennessee. He graduated from Oxford's University High School in 1941. His father John worked as a bridge engineer; he helped build bridges and roads throughout the Delta. Jimmy attended the University of Mississippi, and later, after graduating from the Naval Aviation Cadet Program and completing training, was commissioned in the Marine Air Corps as a pilot. In World War II he flew missions from Okinawa to Japan. In 1947 he obtained a Bachelor of Science degree in engineering. He served again in the Korean War and was awarded the Distinguished Flying Cross. After returning to Oxford, he operated a construction company from 1955 until his retirement in 1983. Jimmy still lives in Oxford with his daughter, Meg Faulkner DuChaine, and her husband, John. His sons, Rusty and Buddy, live in Oxford. His grandchildren are William, Jack, John, and Sarah. Their names echo those of the children in William's generation: William, Jack, John, and cousin Sallie.

Pearle Galloway, or "Miss Pearle," as she is known, is a native of Oxford, Mississippi. Her father owned and ran one of the oldest businesses in the county—a general store. She still possesses a land grant, signed by Martin Van Buren, which deeded the land to a Chickasaw Indian named Noosakahtubby. The land granted eventually came to her father. A businesswoman in her own right, Miss Pearle served the county as owner of this store for thirty years, after she retired from a long career as a grade-school teacher in Oxford, College Hill, Paris, and Philadelphia, Mississippi, as well as in Hardaman County, Tennessee.

Motee Daniel is also a native of Oxford, Mississippi. He has owned various enterprises, including a general store and a roadhouse. A natural humorist, he tells stories of snakebites, bouts with ring- and tape-worm, the cures for these ailments, bootlegging, and problems with his cows and mules. His stories, which delight his visitors, typify the world Faulkner depicts.

Talking About William Faulkner

INTRODUCTION

The vernacular of a place and time is not easily plotted and mapped. The inflections must be heard. William Faulkner listened to and absorbed the voices and accents of those around him. He knew the families of the farmers who worked the land; he listened to the stories of former slaves, or the children or grandchildren of slaves; he talked with heirs of those who settled sizable portions of Lafayette County; and he heard the legends of Confederate soldiers and of tribulations during the Civil War. People lived events and told and retold remembered or half-forgotten stories within shot of Faulkner's ear. These voices are now almost silent.

The interviews recorded here are the voices of a few of the remaining individuals who speak today as they once spoke to Faulkner. Remnants of old Lafayette County—houses, bridges, country stores—may still be found, though they are now rapidly disappearing. The words of these people and the pictures provide contexts that deepen our knowledge of Faulkner's everyday life and clearly enhance an understanding of the world in which Faulkner lived and of which he wrote. The artifacts that archaeologists unearth become much more significant with an understanding of how, when, and why they were made. Similarly, details about the lives of writers enhance understanding of their achievements.

Beginning in the early 1970s and continuing through the 1980s, Floyd C. Watkins and I, both of Emory University, took students of southern literature to Lafayette County to explore Faulkner's region. In caravans we visited Faulkner's home, Rowan Oak, in Oxford, Mississippi; we trekked around the countryside to see and to listen, and we met people who lived the life about which Faulkner wrote. Our guide, spokesman, and witness was Jimmy Faulkner, William's nephew. He agreed to be recorded during these tours, and the first tapes, with true Faulkner élan, were eleven hours in length. After Floyd Watkins retired, I continued the class trips to Oxford for five more years. We combined our interviews for this publication, using tapes that are a part of the Spe-

Fig. 1. Jimmy Faulkner at Rowan Oak (*Photograph by Billy Howard*)

cial Collections at Emory University. Both Watkins and I appreciate and thank the students from Emory University and Arkansas State University who attended these tours.

These interviews are extraordinarily comprehensive and chronicle Jimmy's developing relationship with his uncle. When Jimmy was a small boy, William asked him to call him "Brother Will." His friendship with William grew, particularly in his later years. Jimmy and William shared an enthusiasm for hunting, flying, and five o'clock cocktails. After the deaths of William and his brother John, Jimmy Faulkner became the head of the Faulkner clan. "One day, I spoke up," he says, "and everybody listened."

After William Faulkner's death in 1962, Jimmy became increasingly aware of his uncle's achievement and of what it means to be a Faulkner. In a conscious act of loyalty, Jimmy chose to keep the *u* that William Faulkner had restored to the family name. Today he lives in an antebellum home designed by the architect who built Rowan Oak. He has saved, collected, and preserved family heirlooms, including the dining room table, walking canes, and a pocket watch that belonged to William Faulkner's great-grandfather, Colonel W. C. Falkner. Many of these possessions he keeps in his bedroom, including William Faulkner's RAF wings and flying goggles from World War I. Jimmy also has William's sailing paraphernalia (a compass; a fishing license; the nameplate for his sailing boat, the *Ringdove,* with the letters handstenciled on it by Faulkner; and the sailboat flag with a martini glass embroidered on it). In the gun cabinet next to the bedroom, he keeps William Faulkner's hunting rifles and shotguns (one gun is embossed with a brass plate with the fading initials WF), and he also continues the family tradition of curing meat and canning fruits and vegetables. Jimmy retains a sense of family pride. His storytelling amalgamates his experience with his county and community and his close acquaintance with his uncle's personality. At times his tales seem to mingle fact and fiction. In explaining the origin of the story of Sutpen's Hundred, for example, he perpetuates legends that persist in his region, where people are still tied, however tenuously, to the land and practice customs that are disappearing rapidly.

In these interviews, we move through Lafayette County and encounter the sources of Faulkner's sense of place and its past: people, country stores, mules, dogtrot houses, and wooden ruins of plantation homes built by some of the first settlers. In the town of Oxford, much has also disappeared since Faulkner's death. The old jail is gone, replaced by a modern edifice with less appealing architecture and none of the historical significance of the old jail. The cemeteries remain. Here, free at last, black and white people and people of a mixture of races and cultures achieve a kind of equality. However, some lie in unmarked graves and others beneath large tomb markers and in crypts, some in neglected graves and others in graves well kept. Some names on the tombstones are recognizable, or almost recognizable, from Faulkner's fiction. Some graves belong to slaves who went by their masters' surnames; others show how a master's surname became a slave's first name.

Two colorful local personalities, Pearle Galloway and Motee Daniel, talk about their lives and offer glimpses of the kind of people who fascinated Faulkner. Miss Pearle, who lives in Oxford, owned a general store in College Hill. Although the building remains standing and is visible from the road as evidence of a lost era, her business—with its barrels of pickles, large wheels of cheese, and soda in bottles (deposit required)—is now closed. Miss Pearle's prized possession is the yellowed land grant given to her father. Dated 1836, the deed is signed by Martin Van Buren, granting land to the Native American Noosakahtubby. Miss Pearle has mixed opinions of Faulkner: she praises his community service, but she found him at times impersonal and "very different."

The fading presence of Choctaw and Chickasaw cultures can be found in names of rivers, such as Yoknapatawpha (now Yocona) and Tallahatchie, or creeks, such as Toby Tubby and Puskus. Court records include land deeds transfering Native American homelands to the white settlers. A deed found in the Oxford Courthouse records without elaboration the land transfer of the Old Jones Place from Wee Hun Na Yo to William J. Jones in 1836, but behind such seemingly straightforward transactions lies a history of treaties and negotiations. As Pearle's deed and the transfer of the Jones property attest, residents of the community were not unaware of such land trades. Faulkner, too, made his own record of them in *Go Down, Moses; Requiem for a Nun;* and the Snopes trilogy.

In the talk of Motee Daniel, Pearle Galloway, and Jimmy Faulkner, the vernacular of northern Mississippi surfaces again—in stories of cows, mules, snakes, whisky making, and country stores. Voices of Faulkner's tellers of tales about Yoknapatawpha echo once more. Jimmy Faulkner recounts, as if it were a recent event, the story of Federal troops camping on the lawn of the home he now owns, and he describes a slave mother who left her children in order to escape to the North. Recollecting a story about his Grandma Harkins, who hid her livestock from the Yankees, he adds a layer to the myth of the South much as William Faulkner did with his fiction.

A return to Faulkner's world enlarges the sense of Faulkner's cultural sources and resources and shows more clearly how deeply Faulkner's family, community, and region imprinted themselves on his mind and imagination, and how he was molded and changed by virtually everything that touched him. Two other, related themes emerge in the interviews and reverse the flow of influence. Faulkner, too, changed what he touched: the wide, deep, revisionary impact of Faulkner on his family, his community, and his region becomes apparent. This same revisionary force of his fiction also shapes the ideas of those interviewing and those being interviewed. Faulkner's fiction affects what they look at, how they do their looking, what they see and say. The interviews focus, then, upon ways Faulkner drew upon the historical world of northern Mississippi, but they also disclose how deeply Faulkner's writing has shaped what his relatives, his community, and his readers see, remember, question, and interpret.

In unexpected ways these interviews provide a fuller understanding of what it means to both a family and a community to have "abrupt" upon them, as Faulkner might put it, not simply a writer destined for international fame but also a great writer determined to appropriate and transform the world in a series of stories and novels that have changed forever who they are and how they understand their world. On the other hand, the interest and presence of scholars and students in Mississippi suggest how impossible it is to see that world as a whole except through the lens of Faulkner's fiction.

The world as Faulkner knew it is disappearing rapidly and soon will exist only in literature. The voices Faulkner heard are all but lost, as are the places he knew. Few survivors know who is buried in the unmarked, recessed graves behind the College Hill Church. Fewer still know why they are sunken. What markers remain suffer from the slow but steady erasure of rain. Buildings, too, are in ruins now. Only a few voices still offer testimony. Faulkner, we know, did not seek factual accuracy in fiction. "Facts," he said, "have very little connection with truth." But connections and ties are many, and they enhance our sense of the significance of Faulkner's achievement.

Sally Wolff
Emory University

1

OXFORD HOMES AND SETTINGS

The interviews begin at the gate of William Faulkner's home, Rowan Oak, a place which evokes a southern way of life that influenced Faulkner's imagination. Jimmy Faulkner then discusses his home, which greatly resembles Rowan Oak in appearance and exemplifies the Faulkner family heritage. Moving along toward town, he describes other sites with relevance to Faulkner's fiction, including the Chandler House, a beautiful old southern structure, dreaming now in the shadow of a great magnolia. The Chandler family may have inspired the Compson portrait in The Sound and the Fury. *Jimmy next points out the location of the historical Oxford Jail that stood in the town in Faulkner's time and appeared in his stories, and the Big Ditch, where Nelse Patton ran, as Joe Christmas did in* Light in August. *The last location visited is the University of Mississippi Reading Room, on the college campus, where some of Faulkner's manuscripts are held. Faulkner's presence on the campus endures. His words are engraved in large letters on the side of the library: "I decline to accept the end of man. . . . I believe that man will not merely endure: he will prevail." The first section of the interviews concludes after discussion of the homes and other natural and architectural places in town and their importance in Faulkner's world.*

ROWAN OAK

The window was open, a pear tree grew there, close against the house. It was in bloom and the branches scraped and rasped against the house and the myriad air, driving in the window, brought into the room the forlorn scent of blossoms.

—The Sound and the Fury

Rowan Oak—Faulkner's home and the place where he most often wrote after 1930, when he acquired it—is an antebellum mansion shadowed by towering oaks and cedars.[1] The house epitomizes the sedate, rural, measured pace of Mississippi life—humid and languid summer afternoons and quiet evenings, punctuated by the call of the cicadas from the surrounding trees. Preserved with careful attention to detail, Rowan Oak retains the same stateliness and textures of southern living that it had at the time of Faulkner's death. The house is a haunting reminder of his devotion to home and land, and it bears witness to that mixture of gentility and discipline that nurtured Faulkner's writing life.

Once inside the mansion's columned portico, our guide, William Faulkner's nephew Jimmy, reminisces about his famous uncle. Jimmy and James Webb, curator of Rowan Oak at the time of the first interviews, recall its associations. The barn, the oldest building on the property, is a reminder of the Faulkner family's long equestrian tradition. On the walls of several rooms are paintings by Faulkner's mother, Maud Butler Falkner.[2]

Jimmy looks at an old wine bottle on a shelf and recalls the night of a convivial game supper at which he, William, and a group of friends drained the contents of that very bottle. Mounted in the library are the stuffed game birds that were the prizes of William's many hunting expeditions. Jimmy points to a stuffed owl perched on the mantel. Faulkner discovered the bird poaching his ducks and made it the special target of his next hunt. The library, musty but free of dust, still contains many of the volumes Faulkner collected and read. In Faulkner's office are a desk, lamp, typewriter, and single bed—testaments to the few tools necessary for the writer.

1. On Faulkner's purchase of Rowan Oak, see Joseph Blotner, *Faulkner: A Biography* (2 vols.; New York, 1974), I, 653.

2. "Nanny," Jimmy Faulkner's paternal grandmother. For a full account of the variation in spelling of the Faulkner name, see Appendix A. See also John Faulkner, *my brother Bill: An Affectionate Remembrance* (New York, 1963), 210–11. Hereafter, general references to the Faulkner family name will be spelled with the *u*.

[At the Rowan Oak front gate.]

F. Watkins: Is Rowan Oak one word or two?

J. Faulkner: I've seen it written both ways.[3]

S. Wolff: Did William Faulkner plant these cedars along the drive?

J. Faulkner: No. These cedars were planted when the house was built. They are a hundred and twenty or forty years old, something like that.

S. Wolff: Did he do much gardening?[4]

J. Faulkner: He wasn't interested in anything like lawnmowers and rakes. He didn't do much with the lawn.[5] He wouldn't fill up the ruts in the driveway, either; they would wash out.

S. Wolff: Did Faulkner build this brick wall?

J. Faulkner: Yes. When he'd sit out there in the afternoon, people would drive up and sit and look at him. So he built a wall.[6]

Brother Will[7] also had posts on both sides of the drive here. Cho-Cho,[8] his stepdaughter, wanted a new car. One time she'd come home, she'd hit a post with the old car. The next time she'd bang it on the other. That's what she did. Finally, she knocked all the posts down and pretty

---

3. See Blotner, *Faulkner: A Biography,* I, 660–61. See also David Minter, *William Faulkner: His Life and Work* (Baltimore, 1982), 122.

4. "I'm a farmer. . . . I ain't a writer" (James B. Meriwether and Michael Millgate, eds., *Lion in the Garden: Interviews with William Faulkner, 1926–62* [New York, 1968], 64). Although William Faulkner owned farm land, John Falkner claims William never farmed, although he thought of himself as (in John's term) "a man of the soil" (*my brother Bill,* 242). See also Minter, who notes that Faulkner "realized his dream to becoming a farmer by buying a 320-acre farm that he named Greenfield" (Minter, *William Faulkner,* 176).

5. Minter comments that Estelle, Victoria, and Malcolm helped William with the landscaping of Rowan Oak (Minter, *William Faulkner,* 122). John Falkner points out that "though Bill wasn't mechanically inclined, he did like to piddle about his yard, and bought all sorts of tools for that purpose" (*my brother Bill,* 202).

6. See Floyd C. Watkins, "William Faulkner in His Own Country," *Emory University Quarterly,* XV (1989), 228–39, for a discussion of other measures taken by William Faulkner to discourage visitors.

7. Jimmy Faulkner's familial name for his uncle.

8. Victoria, daughter of Lida Estelle Oldham Franklin and Cornell Franklin.

Fig. 2. Rowan Oak, William Faulkner's home (*Photograph by Billy Howard*)

much wrecked her car. "Well," he said, "that's what you're going to drive." He wouldn't buy another one.[9]

S. Wolff: Was the first building on the property this small log barn?

J. Faulkner: Yes. Indians built it.

S. Wolff: Do you know what year?

J. Faulkner: The house was built in 1848, so the barn must have been built then or before.

S. Wolff: Who constructed the stable?

J. Faulkner: In about 1957, Brother Will wanted to build that stable back there. He couldn't get anyone to help him, so he built it himself. He claimed to be a pretty good carpenter, and he was.

S. Wolff: Do you know what the small log stable is made of and what's in between the logs?

J. Faulkner: The logs had nothing in between them at one time. Brother Will caulked them with cement.

S. Wolff: Oh, I see.

J. Faulkner: The logs were cut with a broad axe. See the marks on it? The stable used to have a tin roof. That's the roof I tried to fly off of one time.[10] I flew five feet out. There was a hedge in this corner. I went through the hedge, upside down, and hung the wings I had made in the tree.

I went barefooted every summer, and Brother Will was reading over there in his west side yard. I was up there on the roof, and my bare feet were burning from the hot tin roof. I got up there and yelled, "Watch me! I am going to fly." He had his back turned, and it was so hot I couldn't stand still in my bare feet, so I started running.

I called out, and he looked and yelled, "Stop—stop, stop!" just about the time I started flying. I hung in that tree. I was so little I could

9. John Falkner said William would keep a car "till the floor boards rusted out of it." After he won the Nobel Prize, all the car dealers in town "[camped] on his door-step" in an attempt to sell him a car. William chose not to buy a new car (*my brother Bill,* 252–53).

10. See Jimmy Faulkner's elaboration of this story, "Solo," in his book *Across the Creek: Faulkner Family Stories* (Jackson, Miss., 1986), 55–60.

have done it, if the wings had been a little bigger. He said, "Don't do that again. If you want to, I'll take you to Memphis tomorrow to fly." So he took four of us up to Memphis in his car, and we flew.

S. Wolff: Did William Faulkner teach you to fly?

J. Faulkner: Well, John,[11] my daddy, taught me to fly, too. When we would go somewhere, he would let me fly after we got in the air. He had planned on me to be the youngest pilot in the United States, but I actually soloed the first time in Fort Smith, Arkansas, when I went in the navy program.

S. Wolff: Did you fly with William Faulkner often?

J. Faulkner: Yes. I did. I'd meet him in Memphis, and we'd fly from there.

[Moving to the side yard.]

This is where I learned how to drink gin and tonics, too. One afternoon in 1954—I had just come back from Korea—we were sitting out here, and Brother Will said, "Have you ever had a gin and tonic?" I said, "No, sir." He said, "I'm going to give you the best summertime drink you ever had." I said, "All right." So he fixed me one, and it was great. I was there at five o'clock every afternoon after that. [Laughter.]

S. Wolff: How old were you when you had your first drink?

J. Faulkner: Fourteen, I believe. That was bad. John and Brother Will were drinking out at the farm.[12] They were drinking straight whiskey—corn whiskey—out of a tin cup. I was going from the house down to the barn to catch a horse and go riding. I walked past them, and Brother Will called out to me and said: "You're old enough now to have your first drink, and we want you to have your first drink with us." I said, "All right." So they had this tin cup, poured corn whiskey in it, and said, "Here."

Now, I had seen them drink, so I started drinking all of it at once. I couldn't breathe for a minute after that, and it burned my stomach. I finally got up the hill—it was all I could do. I couldn't get into bed or any-

11. John Wesley Thompson Falkner III asked Jimmy to call him "John."
12. Greenfield Farm.

thing. My mother[13] knew what had happened, and she called my grand-mother. This caused a split in the family: nobody would talk to John or me, and Nanny wouldn't let me come down to Brother Will's house by myself. I guess it was a year before things finally settled down. It took me a long time to sober up, too. [Laughter.] That corn whiskey was two hundred proof; that's pure alcohol!

S. Wolff: Did William Faulkner drink corn whiskey often?

J. Faulkner: Brother Will drank what was cheap and available. Mississippi was dry then. He drank Jack Daniels when it came available. Brother Will claimed to have introduced Jack Daniels to Virginia. Dean Martin introduced it to the West Coast. [Laughter.]

S. Wolff: I've noticed two snakes around this house so far.

J. Faulkner: One day Brother Will and I were sitting out here in chairs with our feet up on the front porch rail, and this snake crawled by me. I jumped and screamed, "Get that damn snake away from me!" I was going to kill it when Brother Will said, "Don't you touch Penelope." It was his pet snake, but I just wanted to keep that thing away from me![14]

S. Wolff: How long did he have the pet snake?

J. Faulkner: A long time—years—too damn long; I didn't like it. It was a rat snake. It ate rats. Brother Will never picked it up. It kept the rats away from the house. Brother Will didn't bother it, and it didn't bother him.

[Looking at a vine-covered arbor in William Faulkner's back yard.]

S. Wolff: This is a muscadine, isn't it?

J. Faulkner: No, it's a golden scuppernong, a cousin to the dark purple muscadine; this scuppernong is golden and sweeter.

S. Wolff: What do you prepare out of this golden one?

J. Faulkner: You can make wine or jams out of it.

13. Jimmy Faulkner's mother, Lucille "Dolly" Ramey Falkner, like her husband John, asked Jimmy to call her by her first name.

14. For a similar reaction by William Faulkner upon an early encounter with a snake, see Faulkner, *my brother Bill,* 42–43.

Fig. 3. Scuppernong vines in the side yard at Rowan Oak
(*Photograph by Billy Howard*)

S. Wolff: Is there a pear tree against the side of his house like the one Miss Quentin climbed down in *The Sound and the Fury?*

J. Faulkner: No, but I do have a pear tree at my house and a rain pipe. This house has a rain pipe, too, and that tree is close to the house, but it is not a pear tree.

[In Rowan Oak's front yard.]

J. Faulkner: Brother Will bought this house after he and Aunt Estelle married.[15] I guess my family's a bunch of nomads. We never really stayed in one house the whole time.

My first bull ride was right here. Brother Will had a six-month-old bull that he kept tied right out here so it could graze. He had just returned from California with his stepson, Malcolm,[16] who was about five

15. William and Estelle Faulkner married in June, 1929, and moved into Rowan Oak in 1930. See Blotner, *Faulkner: A Biography,* I, 657; Minter, *William Faulkner,* 121; and Faulkner, *my brother Bill,* 160–62, for discussions of the purchase of Rowan Oak.

16. Malcolm Argyle Franklin.

Fig. 4. The original kitchen off the back of the house at Rowan Oak. Such kitchens were constructed to remove the dangerous and intense cooking fires and accompanying heat from the main domicile. (*Photograph by Billy Howard*)

months younger than I am. Brother Will brought me back a cowboy hat from one of those specialty stores. John, my daddy, said, "Since you've got this hat, I'll get you a pair of spurs." I went barefooted everywhere in the summer, and I wore the spurs barefooted. John said I was the only cowboy he ever saw who wore spurs barefooted.

The bull was tied on a rope to a stake. I said, "Malcolm, if you can hold that bull while I get on it, I'll ride it." The bull was still tied to a stake by a rope, so I got on it. I tipped my hat, like they do in cowboy shows when the cowboy hits the bull with the hat. I hit the bull and spurred him at the same time, and the first thing the bull did was to run over Malcolm.

We then came to the end of the rope. The bull stopped, but I didn't. I skidded off the bull to the right. Brother Will saw what we were doing and came out. I said, "If that bull hadn't been tied, I could've ridden it." He said, "All right, I'm going to show you how to do it." So he got a rope and tied it around the bull's chest. He said, "Now, you don't need spurs." So I took them off. He said, "You're going to lose your hat, anyway," so he took it off of me.

Brother Will placed my hands real tight in that rope, and he got my feet in the rope, too. All of my toes were sticking out from the bull. Brother Will turned that bull loose. [Pointing.] Under that vine, there was a blackberry bush about twenty feet across and about four feet high. A part of the vine was hanging just low enough to catch me in the throat. The bull kept going. The vine pulled so hard—it bent some limbs up there—it finally snatched me off the bull, and I fell backward and got caught in the blackberry bush.

Brother Will came and got me loose. He said, "It looks like somebody hung you." I said, "You and that bull did!" We spent the rest of the morning picking briars out of my toes. He said, "Now, that's enough," and I said, "I think so." [Laughter.]

[Inside Rowan Oak.]

J. Faulkner: [To James Webb.[17]] How are you getting along?

J. Webb: Fine. Please come in and look around.

S. Wolff: The house is remarkably cool.

J. Faulkner: The family wanted it cool. They would open up a back door and let the breeze blow through.

S. Wolff: Is the wallpaper original?

J. Faulkner: I'm not sure.

S. Wolff: This bedroom was Faulkner's bedroom. That one down the hall was Estelle's?

J. Faulkner: Right. When I would stay with Brother Will, he let me stay in his room, and he would go someplace else and stay.

S. Wolff: Like other large homes with high ceilings, this one has no air conditioners—only one, in Estelle's room.

J. Faulkner: Brother Will didn't like air conditioning; there's one air conditioner in the house, and it's in Aunt Estelle's room. He did like to stay warm, though; he didn't go without heat.[18]

17. Curator at Rowan Oak at the time of one interview in 1980.
18. Faulkner had a central heating system installed in Rowan Oak (Faulkner, *my brother Bill,* 264).

Fig. 5. William Faulkner's bedroom at Rowan Oak (*Photograph by Billy Howard*)

J. Webb: The furniture has been taken to a warehouse during the restoration, but you can use your imagination. Seeing the house gives some ideas about how William Faulkner lived.

S. Wolff: When he bought this house, it was in disrepair, wasn't it?

J. Faulkner: Oh, yes.[19]

S. Wolff: He didn't buy it for a whole lot of money, did he?

J. Faulkner: No, it wasn't much.[20]

S. Wolff: Then he slowly refurbished it over the years?

J. Faulkner: Yes. The first thing he did was to put a beam under the house. He and Rusty Patterson,[21] a good painter and carpenter in town, crawled under the house with a fifth of whiskey and installed the

19. Among other things, Rowan Oak needed electricity, water, new wiring, plumbing, new floor beams, a new roof, and painting (*ibid.*, 162).

20. See Blotner, *Faulkner: A Biography,* I, 653.

21. An occasional drinking companion of William Faulkner's. See *ibid.*, 558, 657, for further details.

beam. When they crawled out from under the house, they were both drunk, but the beam was in place.[22]

S. Wolff: Did William Faulkner do the rest of the renovations?

J. Faulkner: He helped a lot. Brother Will did a lot because he didn't have any money then. But as he got a little money, he would add things.[23]

S. Wolff: Who played the piano?

J. Faulkner: Aunt Estelle. She was pretty good.

S. Wolff: Did you live here in Rowan Oak for a while?

J. Faulkner: Yes. I lived at Rowan Oak in the front room when I was in the ninth grade.

S. Wolff: Why did you stay here then?

J. Faulkner: Brother Will had just bought a farm, and my daddy ran it for him.[24] I had to live at Rowan Oak so I could go to school in town. I also used to spend every weekend there, even when I moved from town out to this farm my daddy ran. But when I played high school football for three years, I stayed in town. I spent other nights with Brother Will so we could get up early and go duck hunting the next day. Sometimes I stayed the night just for the hell of it.

S. Wolff: When you stayed here, what did you do in the evenings?

J. Faulkner: Brother Will used to read to us at night—*Robinson Crusoe,* I think. There's a place where we used to have weenie roasts and marshmallow roasts, and he would make up a story and tell it to us. He would start the story with everyone sitting around the campfire. Each person would add a little to it, and he would finish it. I was ten or twelve years of age at the time.

S. Wolff: What else did he like to take with him?

J. Faulkner: I do remember that he didn't take a radio with him to these campfires.

---

22. See Faulkner, *my brother Bill,* 162–63, for a similar recounting of the story. See also Blotner, *Faulkner: A Biography,* I, 657–58.

23. See Faulkner, *my brother Bill,* 162–63, for corroboration.

24. Greenfield Farm was purchased in 1938 (Minter, *William Faulkner,* 176–77). See also Faulkner, *my brother Bill,* 176–90, for John Falkner's account of running William's farm.

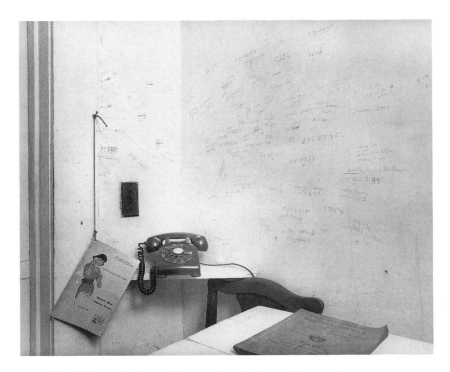

Fig. 6. The telephone table near the kitchen at Rowan Oak. William Faulkner wrote the names and phone numbers of friends and acquaintances on the wall. (*Photograph by Billy Howard*)

S. Wolff: Where did William hold the weenie roasts?

J. Faulkner: Down behind the stable at Rowan Oak—in a sand ditch.

[In the kitchen.]

S. Wolff: [Looking at the wall near the telephone.] Are these numbers written on the wall in William Faulkner's handwriting?

J. Faulkner: Yes. Brother Will wrote the numbers of his relatives and a few friends on this wall. That was his directory for the phone. Now, that's real organization, isn't it?

S. Wolff: Did he think of the telephone as an intrusion?

J. Faulkner: Intrusion? Yes.

S. Wolff: Was William Faulkner opposed to other modern conveniences?

J. Faulkner: He said he didn't like appliances meddling in his life. Brother Will did not like TV or radio, but he did tolerate the telephone and did read the paper.[25] One time I brought a radio and sneaked it into the house in my hunting jacket. I put it under my pillow and listened to it in bed. Brother Will never knew!

[Moving through Rowan Oak and observing the rooms in which William Faulkner lived and worked.]

J. Webb: Some of Maud's oil paintings were put in the museum where they will get proper environment with moisture control. They began restoration, supposedly, August 7.[26] We've hired an archivist, three architects, a contractor, an assistant, a foreman, and two workmen to do the job.

The restoration was supposed to be completed by March, but you can't be too optimistic; there have been problems.[27] We hired some people out of Washington, D.C., to scrape paint. According to their analysis, this house has been painted sixteen times on the outside—I don't know how many times on the inside. They're trying to use the same paint that they used back about 1960 or thereabouts.[28]

F. Watkins: What did Oxford provide your uncle as a writer?

J. Faulkner: The bases for a lot of his stories are the older people in our family who passed down legends and stories that he heard over

25. According to Blotner, William Faulkner was adamant about not buying a television or radio; however, he did have a favorite television program (Blotner, *Faulkner: A Biography,* II, 1812).

26. Restoration began in August, 1979.

27. With restoration completed in the summer of 1980, Rowan Oak opened officially to the public on August 3, 1980.

28. Jimmy Faulkner recalls that, upon seeing the pinkish paint that the architect chose to match the original color, he exclaimed that the house had always been white. "The last time Brother Will painted it before he died," Jimmy insists, "I came over and said I'd get enough paint for us both, so I could paint my house, too. I remember what kind of paint it was: Burke Hall outside white. The paint analyst must have taken a chip off the lower part of the house where the mud has splashed up into the house wall. That would have given the paint that reddish tinge."

and over again. Before radio and TV, there would be three generations of family in the same house—and possibly four.

S. Wolff: How did the residents of Oxford react to William Faulkner's receiving the Nobel Prize?

J. Faulkner: Many in Oxford didn't know what that prize was or what he did to get it.[29]

William Faulkner's office, sparsely furnished,[30] contains a manual typewriter on the writing table, a single bed, a small bookcase, an extra chair, and the famous outline of his novel A Fable, *which he sketched on the wall beside his bed. The senses detect the smell of a space no longer occupied.*

J. Faulkner: This is the room Brother Will called his office. He enclosed this part of the back gallery in 1952 and made the office. He did most of his writing up until then in the front room, called the library. After that he wrote in the office. Brother Will would sit here at his typewriter and look out the window.

S. Wolff: Why did William Faulkner write on this wall?

J. Faulkner: Brother Will never kept notes. When he started writing *A Fable,* it got out of hand. It took him ten years to do it, so he did keep notes. He stacked them beneath the days of the week that he had written on the wall here.

When he thought he was through, he left word with James Fitchett, the painter, to paint the wall. Brother Will then went to Greenville to see Ben Wasson,[31] and he remembered that he had forgotten something to put in the novel. He beat it back up here to stop the painter, but Mr. Fitchett had already painted over the notes. A painter never does anything on time except this one time!

29. Minter argues that Oxford residents were impressed by "stories you could read in beauty parlors and barbershops," not by "poems full of nymphs and fauns and novels about perverts and idiots" (Minter, *William Faulkner,* 123).

30. William Faulkner's needs were simple: "solitude, pencil, and paper; tobacco, food, and whiskey" (*ibid.,* 240).

31. Faulkner's lifelong friend from the University of Mississippi who, from 1928 on, acted as his literary agent. See Blotner, *Faulkner: A Biography,* I, 563, II, 1463, for further details.

Fig. 7. William Faulkner's typewriter (*Photograph by Billy Howard*)

Fig. 8. The single bed in William Faulkner's office where he often stayed. Still visible on the wall is the outline he wrote for his novel *A Fable*. (*Photograph by Billy Howard*)

Then Brother Will remembered that Bern Keating, a photographer, had taken pictures of the wall with the notes on it.[32] He got Bern Keating's pictures, copied the notes back on the wall in indelible ink,[33] and then shellacked that part of the wall so it couldn't be painted over again. He put "Tomorrow"[34] appropriately behind the door where you are.

J. Webb: The writing on the walls is still here. That varnish has turned darker by the year. I suppose the gas heat helped it along. It was quite obvious to the authorities who were looking at it that in time it would be rather difficult to read it. Another expert from New Orleans, a

32. A photographer who traveled to Oxford to photograph the outline of *A Fable* that Faulkner had written on the walls of his study. See *ibid.*, II, 1465–66, for corroboration.

33. According to Howard Bahr, who was curator of Rowan Oak from 1984 to 1993, the outline is written in red grease pencil and black carpenter's pencil (Howard Bahr to Sally Wolff, September 12, 1991).

34. Part of the outline of the novel *A Fable*.

Fig. 9. The chair in the library at Rowan Oak in which William Faulkner often sat and wrote (*Photograph by Billy Howard*)

Mrs. Huxley, whose expertise is in restoring oil paintings, used something like a little toothbrush and some kind of solvent. She was able to remove all of that varnish off the edge.

[In the library.]

J. Faulkner: Until about 1952, he wrote in the library in that corner over there, where that lamp is so that he could look out over his left shoulder. When I was little, we'd play outside, and he would get more interested in what we were doing than his writing. He would come out there and play with us.

That wine bottle up there on the shelf—let me tell you about that. In the late fifties, Mississippi was dry. I went to Memphis a good bit. When we had a game supper at his house, Brother Will would say: "Bring us back two bottles of wine, one to drink and one to cook with." One of the bottles that I brought back to drink he took and put inside that rail in front of the fireplace to draw heat from the fire. Then he would take the birds that were cooked in wine and come back in here and serve it with the warm wine.

We hunted quail in Holly Springs with some of my friends on horseback with dogs. When the dogs would point, we'd get off the horses and shoot. My friends had around three thousand acres. One time we'd killed a good many birds, so Brother Will invited these friends to Oxford for a quail supper a few nights later. He asked me to get the wine to cook the quail with.

There were about six of us. I brought that bottle and another one like it, and he set the bottle of wine by the fire here in the library to get warm. We had a drink and finished the bird supper. We then sat around the fire and drank the bottle of fire-heated wine. If you think that can't get to you quick—oh! [Laughter.] That one bottle, and there were six of us just sitting there enjoying it by the fire.

S. Wolff: Did William Faulkner do the cooking after quail hunts?

J. Faulkner: No, but he did cook his own breakfast.

S. Wolff: What would he fix for breakfast?

J. Faulkner: His favorite breakfast was either buttered toast and orange marmalade or bacon, eggs, and toast.[35] He loved orange marmalade. He would fix hot chocolate for me, and he would have coffee. He thought I was too young for coffee, but I was old enough at fourteen years of age to take my first drink of corn whiskey!

S. Wolff: Did you and your uncle often eat together?

J. Faulkner: Brother Will would go out and buy salmon, and he would make salmon croquettes. We would pour a lot of catsup over them and eat them until we were sick. They were great.

S. Wolff: Maud painted the paintings hanging in most of the rooms, didn't she?

J. Faulkner: Yes. Nanny sold a lot of paintings. She could do two a day. Brother Will and my daddy both just picked it up from her.[36] Now, she painted that magnolia picture, this picture of the Old Colonel, and that picture of Brother Will when he was about thirty years old. My grandmother didn't have a frame to fit the picture, so she just painted the appearance of a frame onto the bottom of the picture.

Nanny was such a frugal person. She wouldn't let anything go to waste. For a fire screen over the fireplace in the summer, she used a Coca-Cola sign and painted a vase of flowers on it.

S. Wolff: Was your father also frugal?

J. Faulkner: Oh, no. John, my daddy, was extravagant. Dolly got mad at John when I was born. He had twenty dollars, and after I was born he took the twenty dollars, went to town, and bought some riding boots for himself.

S. Wolff: Would you say William Faulkner was frugal or extravagant?

35. John Falkner corroborates that William Faulkner regularly prepared this same breakfast of bacon, eggs, toast, and coffee for his mother (*my brother Bill*, 266).

36. Maud Butler Falkner painted several of the portraits and other pictures now hanging in Rowan Oak and in Jimmy Faulkner's home. John Falkner stated that "our talent to draw and paint came from [our grandmother]. Mother inherited it and passed it on to Bill and me and Dean" (*ibid.*, 123).

J. Faulkner: Frugal to the point when he didn't have any money, he would type new stories on the back side of pages of old stories that he had already typed.[37]

When the accelerator pedal in his car broke off the stub, he got a broomstick and used his right hand for the accelerator stick. His touring car also had a leaky canvas top, and we had to put on raincoats to ride in it. When the brakes wore out in his car, he needed someone to pull the emergency brake for him. Jill[38] used to do this. He drove that car for probably thirteen or fourteen years until Nanny made him stop riding in it with Jill because it was dangerous. It was an old Ford he bought new. He drove it to California twice.

He also didn't care a whole lot about dress-up clothes. He wore his trench coat until it was threadbare. But when it came to horses and hunting, he bought the best. He was also real generous with people.

S. Wolff: Would you explain the other objects here?

J. Faulkner: That photograph up there is of Brother Will in his riding suit. He brought back the bust of Don Quixote over here from South America. I met him at the airport one night, and I didn't know he was going to bring back a bust. When he walked out with it, I said, "That thing is not going to fit in the airplane." We tried, and it wouldn't fit. He went back to the terminal and had it sent down here air freight. The birds are stuffed. That owl used to catch his ducks, so he killed it and had it stuffed.

Brother Will got a real bad burn on his back while in New York some time around 1937. He fell down and got wedged between a steam pipe and a wall. He thought that sitting in front of the fire would draw the heat off, so he would take his shirt off and sit on that rail and expose his back to the fire.[39]

---

37. See Blotner, *Faulkner: A Biography,* II, 1777, for additional examples of Faulkner's frugality.

38. Jill Faulkner Summers, the daughter of Estelle and William Faulkner.

39. See Minter, *William Faulkner,* 170, and Blotner, *Faulkner, A Biography,* II, 1435.

S. Wolff: I have also heard that cold steel can draw out heat. When I was little, they used to put a cold steel knife on burns and bee stings.

J. Faulkner: Well, I'll be.

[In the living room.]

That's where the casket rested when Brother Will died. We had a service here in the living room. Mammy Callie's[40] was here, too, and he held her service.

S. Wolff: Didn't he deliver her funeral sermon?

J. Faulkner: Yes, right here.

F. Watkins: Now, a few years ago, in a broom closet under a stairway, a part of the *As I Lay Dying* manuscript was found, wasn't it?[41]

J. Webb: We did find some manuscripts in a huge cardboard box. A number of these pieces had been published, like *Sartoris* and some of the others. But what is interesting about those is that you have the original manuscript or the handwritten version, and then you have the revised version of that; then you have a typewritten copy of the publisher, or the typist, or whoever is setting up the type. As you may recall, Mr. Faulkner said on occasion that writing is hard work,[42] even for a man who has a genius and talent for writing. But he didn't just sit down and dash off something.

I think Jimmy would agree with me; for example, one of the earlier books that he wrote was *The Unvanquished,* and a number of pieces in that collection could have served as chapters in *The Unvanquished.* He didn't use them, presumably because he had enough continuity and

40. Caroline "Callie" Barr, born in slavery in the 1840s, lived and worked with the Faulkners. She became a beloved figure in William Faulkner's life, and he dedicated *Go Down, Moses* to her. See Minter, *William Faulkner,* 122, for further details.

41. These papers were found in a broom closet under the front stairs in 1971 by a graduate student named Beverly Smith. The catalog in the Mississippi Collection at the University of Mississippi reveals that the box contained a variety of material, including drafts of *Sanctuary, Absalom, Absalom!, As I Lay Dying,* "Once Aboard the Lugger," "Lizards in Jamshyd's Courtyard," "Golden Land," and "The Brooch" (Bahr to Wolff, September 12, 1991).

42. See, for example, William Faulkner, "An Introduction to *The Sound and the Fury,*" ed. James B. Meriwether, *Southern Review,* VIII (Autumn, 1972), 705–10.

enough of a story without including them. Some of them have characters, similar actions, what not, that remind you of stories that appear in *The Unvanquished.*

F. Watkins: Where are those papers now?

J. Webb: They are in the vault at Ole Miss.

F. Watkins: They will be at Ole Miss rather than the University of Virginia?[43]

J. Webb: Well, that will depend on Jill; they're hers.

F. Watkins: I see.

JIMMY FAULKNER'S HOUSE

I looked at him, watched him fill both glasses. . . . "I am tired of killing men, no matter what the necessity nor the end. Tomorrow, when I go to town and meet Ben Redmond, I shall be unarmed."

—*The Unvanquished*

When Jimmy Faulkner's home and grounds come into view, William Faulkner's literary images come readily to mind. Honeysuckle winds its way through his garden; sparrows and mockingbirds appear in the pear and plum orchard; and rain pipes, much like the one from which Miss Quentin descended, frame the sides of the large antebellum house that closely resembles William Faulkner's. The two houses, in fact, were designed by the same architect.

Jimmy introduces his daughter, Meg Faulkner DuChaine, and discusses her horsemanship in the show ring, a hobby linking her with what William Faulkner called a "family heritage."[44] A brief stop by the gun cabinet reveals several hunting rifles and other guns, at least one owned by William Faulkner. Both a part of the southern hunting tradition, William Faulkner and Jimmy hunted together, uncle introducing nephew to his first rabbit hunt with a rabbit stick (a crude hunting device) for a weapon. An old, burled oak table occupies the center of the dining room. At one such table in The Unvanquished *Colonel Sartoris sat, twirling his wineglass and vowing to fight his last duel without firearms. Other furniture in the hall and dining room belonged to the Old Colonel.*

43. The papers are now the property of the University of Mississippi.
44. Meriwether and Millgate, eds., *Lion in the Garden,* 139.

Fig. 10. Jimmy Faulkner's house, designed by the same architect who built William Faulkner's (*Photograph by Billy Howard*)

Jimmy Faulkner's bookcase contains several of William Faulkner's first editions. Jimmy, however, keeps his autographed first editions under lock and key. The longer Jimmy stands near the bookcase, the more family mementos he displays: from one drawer he produces William Faulkner's fishing license and tackle box; from another, a boat pennant with a martini glass emblem and the signboard from Faulkner's sailboat, the Ringdove. *From his bedroom drawer he brings out two antique pocket watches belonging to a long line of Faulkners. A gallery of portraits of the male Faulkners angles down the slope of the staircase. Jimmy describes his place in the family line and his feelings about these men, most of whom appear in William Faulkner's work in various fictional incarnations.*

[In Jimmy Faulkner's front yard.]

F. Watkins: When was this house built, Jimmy?

J. Faulkner: 1850. I've lived here twenty-five years, I think.

F. Watkins: What's your daughter's name?

J. Faulkner: Meg.[45] Meg was born in the Oxford hospital and still lives in the same room here where she grew up.

F. Watkins: Does she still enter horse show competitions?

J. Faulkner: Yes, but she hasn't since last July. The horse she rode then was the best horse she ever had. This horse, the one that's coming along now, is just fine. This is a tough horse.

F. Watkins: Trained?

J. Faulkner: No. Not yet. Maybe in another six months we'll start.

F. Watkins: How many horses did you say you had at one time?

J. Faulkner: Twenty-something.

F. Watkins: Do you make or lose money?

J. Faulkner: Lose, lose. [Laughter.] The only people who make money off horses are trainers and traders.

F. Watkins: That sounds like some of Faulkner's stories.[46]

J. Faulkner: That's the truth.

[Meg Faulkner DuChaine arrives. She and her husband, John DuChaine, live with her father. She has inherited the Faulkner love of horse training and riding.]

F. Watkins: Hi, Meg. You remember me?

M. Faulkner: No, sir. [Laughter.]

F. Watkins: You going to start riding in horse shows again?

M. Faulkner: No, sir, I'm not going to. Maybe I'll do another show sometime.

S. Wolff: Your family has always loved horses, haven't they?

J. Faulkner: Yes. The Old Colonel's horse was named Pompous.

S. Wolff: Why do you think your family has had such an interest in horsemanship?

J. Faulkner: We all like horses. I guess it's the sense of animal power, just as the airplane gives you a sense of mechanical power. The faster you can go, the better.

45. Margaret Lucille Faulkner DuChaine.
46. *E.g.,* "Spotted Horses" or *The Hamlet.*

F. Watkins: This is the kind of honeysuckle vine that Quentin so often smelled.[47] Who originally built this home?

J. Faulkner: Yancey Wiley.[48] [Birds singing.]

F. Watkins: Got any scuppernongs?

J. Faulkner: No.

S. Wolff: Do you cure your own meat in this smokehouse?[49]

J. Faulkner: Yes. We put it in salt. We have a salt box. It's in an old log house. Salt it down for about a week; bury it in the salt, really. Then brush the salt off and smoke it over hickory logs until it gets about the color of mahogany saddle leather. That takes about a week.

S. Wolff: So then you hang the meat up after it's cured?

J. Faulkner: Yes. It just hangs.

S. Wolff: How long does it stay that way?

J. Faulkner: Forever. If you cure it good and smoke it right, it will stay a long, long time. I take one out every now and then and slice it.

S. Wolff: How many fruit trees do you have?

J. Faulkner: About twenty-five: six plum, five apple, four peach, three pear, two crabapple, one pecan, and six grapevines. That's about it. Whatever that adds up to be. At night I sit next to the window in the bedroom or in the den and listen to the soft sound of the plums falling from the trees and hitting the ground.

S. Wolff: I noticed as we passed through the kitchen that you are making gallons of plum jelly. The kitchen counter tops were lined with hot jars of jelly. Do you also make your own grape jelly?[50]

J. Faulkner: And apple jelly. Freeze apples to make apple cobbler and freeze peaches to make peach preserves. We put peach brandy in them. We grow most of our own vegetables, too.

47. In *The Sound and the Fury,* Quentin Compson associated the smell of honeysuckle with desire and death.

48. An Oxford citizen and first owner of Jimmy Faulkner's home.

49. William Faulkner also maintained a smokehouse and cured his own meat (Faulkner, *my brother Bill,* 238).

50. "Estelle, believing as Bill did in old customs, put up canned foods and jellies and preserves from their own garden and orchards" (*ibid.*). According to Jimmy, William did not help with the canning, although he did like to watch his daughter Jill do so.

Jimmy introduces James and Nat Avant, who both worked for the Faulkner family for almost fifty years. James's heritage—part black and part Chickasaw Indian—closely parallels that of Sam Fathers in "The Bear."

J. Faulkner: I want you to meet Nat and James Avant. James worked for Brother Will from about 1938 to 1947, and Sam Fathers is probably a good deal like him.[51] James's father, Perk Avant, was born a slave. James's mother was an Indian.

When the Federal troops came through, Perk's mother, along with a bunch of other people, followed the troops out, as in *The Unvanquished*. She left Perk, who was fourteen at the time, and his baby sister in a cabin. Perk and his sister went up to the big house on the Avant place, and Perk told Mr. Avant what had happened. The Avants took them in. Mr. Avant said they could stay there and that they would help them.

Perk, like a lot of the slaves did at the end of the war, took on the name of the master. Perk married a half-Indian, half-black woman, making James, his son, one-fourth Indian.

S. Wolff: Mrs. Avant, thank you for the wonderful lunch you fixed [of black-eyed peas, squash, turnip greens, and corn bread]. Mr. Avant, Jimmy said you used to hunt with William Faulkner.

J. Avant: Yes, we hunted many times. I enjoyed hunting with him. I've known and been associated with the Faulkner family for many years.

S. Wolff: How long have you worked for them?

N. Avant: Around fifty years.

J. Faulkner: James can track almost anything—if a horse gets out, he can track it. He also has such stealth in the woods: I'll be thinking he's somewhere a mile off from me, and the next moment he'll be standing behind me, whispering in my ear. He can take me completely by surprise. James also will not eat tame meat. He only eats squirrel, rabbit, venison, and wild turkey.

51. See "The Old People" in *Go Down, Moses* for the story of Sam Fathers, who teaches Ike McCaslin to live and hunt in the woods.

S. Wolff: Do you remember any particularly good stories about hunting with William Faulkner?

J. Avant: No, we just always had a good time.

S. Wolff: It is good to meet you. [The Avants depart.] Jimmy, when did you first hunt with William Faulkner?

J. Faulkner: I started hunting with Brother Will when I was nine or ten. We used a rabbit stick.

S. Wolff: What's a rabbit stick?[52]

J. Faulkner: A stick about three feet long with a bolt screwed on it to give it weight. We would take our dogs, Queenie and Bessie, to flush the rabbits out, and then we would throw the stick and try to hit the rabbits.[53]

S. Wolff: How often did you go hunting with your uncle?

J. Faulkner: When I was a child, often, and later nearly every day.

S. Wolff: What kind of hunting did you do?

J. Faulkner: Quail and ducks, doves, and things like that. Wing shooting. Of course, Brother Will hunted his first deer down in the deer camp. He didn't hunt deer around here.

I was fascinated with quail hunting. I killed my first bird when I was twelve years old. Brother Will would come get me, and we would hunt after school and all day on Saturday. I went to deer camps with him once a year, except when I was away for eight years because of the wars.

When I was in high school, he would ask me to go hunting, and I would say, "Yes, sir." When I got back from Korea, and he had gotten everything settled in California so he didn't have to be out there as much, we would hunt every day. I would drop everything I was doing to go hunting with Brother Will.

S. Wolff: Did you do any bear hunting?

J. Faulkner: The bears were gone before I was old enough to hunt, so I hunted deer as a boy. Brother Will and I never traveled very much.

52. Aleck Sander employs one such weapon in *Intruder in the Dust.*
53. See Blotner, *Faulkner: A Biography,* II, 920, for a different account of rabbit hunting.

He did a lot of his traveling in the front yard.[54] He was like Big Dad,[55] my granddaddy. When mother and daddy first married, Big Dad would talk in a dialect, and he had my mother, Dolly, built up about a steamboat trip down the Mississippi River. Dolly got all excited and talked about it until finally my father said, "Don't you know Dad's traveling is done in the front yard? He's never been out of the front yard."

S. Wolff: Your father said that about his father?

J. Faulkner: About his daddy? Yes.

One time Brother Will wanted to go hunting on a Sunday afternoon. We had a party the night before, and I had a God-awful hangover the next morning. But I had to go. We got to Holly Springs, and I was hoping that we wouldn't find any birds and wouldn't have to shoot because I knew the sound would hurt my head. Well, they gave me a horse, but I don't think it had any water the night before. That horse stopped at every mudhole and drank water, and I constantly got behind the other hunters.

Well, I got to a ditch. There was a sapling right in the middle, and the horse jumped. I saw my left knee was going to hit the sapling, so I kicked it out of the stirrup, but it still hit me right on the kneecap. It hurt! I got up and finally caught up with them. Brother Will laughed and said, "Too much Scotch last night, wasn't it?" And I said, "Yes, sir."

But he didn't think much about Scotch drinking. He liked bourbon. Thought I was a traitor. I would go off to some place and bring back a bottle of Jack Daniels for him. He'd say, "This is going to be some good sippin'." He'd go on a trip and bring me back a bottle of Scotch and just say, "Here."

S. Wolff: Did Big Dad like to hunt?

J. Faulkner: Loved it. He had a setter that had puppies. He built a frame around the fireplace, put blankets in front of it, and sat the dog and the puppies in front of it also. Everybody else had to go into the other room to get warm.

54. John Falkner comments that "Bill liked to talk hunting almost as much as he liked hunting itself" (*my brother Bill,* 199).

55. Murry Cuthbert Falkner, William Faulkner's father.

S. Wolff: Did he teach William to hunt?

J. Faulkner: All four of the boys.

S. Wolff: Did William also hunt with the Young Colonel?

J. Faulkner: The Young Colonel died in 1922. Brother Will was twenty-five when he was seventy-four. So, yes, when they were old enough to hunt with him, they did. Big Dad and Uncle John[56] also hunted with the Young Colonel regularly.

S. Wolff: How far back does hunting go in your family?

J. Faulkner: Falconer—which means hunter—was the spelling of our family name in England, and this goes back to the 1600s.

[Inside Jimmy's house.]

J. Faulkner: Some of my family paintings are in here. This was painted by my daddy: "The Bear" [57]—right there, and "Weighing In" is right there.

S. Wolff: Stark Young[58] lived here for a while, didn't he?

J. Faulkner: He lived right next door to us—my grandmother, mother, and daddy—on University Avenue. I'm told he stayed here, where I am living now, before I lived here, in the summertime in the 1920s. He stayed upstairs in the bedroom on the left-hand side, and he would walk out onto the veranda and stand there, looking out. He said he was practicing elocution and would go out on the balcony and speak to the trees. The servants thought he was crazy.

S. Wolff: Did you hear him do that?

56. John Wesley Thompson Falkner, Jr. ("Uncle John").

57. John, a writer and an artist (like his mother), painted subjects of local color interest. John stated that William offered him five hundred dollars "to execute" two scenes from "The Bear" and "Red Leaves" on the wall of his study. John painted the watercolors, but William never reproduced them on his wall (Faulkner, *my brother Bill,* 175).

58. Born in Como, Mississippi, in 1881, Stark Young graduated in 1901 from the University of Mississippi with a Bachelor of Arts degree in English and in 1904 returned to Ole Miss as a professor of rhetoric and literature. Young was also a poet, playwright, drama critic, Broadway director, novelist, translator, and painter. See John Pilkington, *Stark Young* (Boston, 1985).

Fig. 11. A sideboard in Jimmy Faulkner's house, much like the one described in *The Sound and the Fury* (*Photograph by Billy Howard*)

J. Faulkner: No, but Mr. Ed Newman, the man I bought my house from, told me about it. I was only with Stark Young three or four times when he came down and presented papers at Ole Miss. I don't even know how old he was because he was up in years by then.

F. Watkins: Stark Young was the author of the best seller *So Red the Rose.*

[Moving to Jimmy's den, Watkins points to the guns and rifles
in the cabinet.]

F. Watkins: What's the oldest gun here?

J. Faulkner: The two on the bottom. One of these is a .41-caliber Lightning revolver like gamblers—card players—used to carry under the shoulder, and the other one is just an old Peacemaker.

F. Watkins: You don't have a derringer, do you?

J. Faulkner: No, I don't. Wish I had the Old Colonel's. Everyone said he was the best. The gun next to the bottom was Brother Will's bird gun.

F. Watkins: Double-barrel, one barrel over the other?

J. Faulkner: Yes.

F. Watkins: How old is that gun?

J. Faulkner: He had it made in about 1935 or 1936.

F. Watkins: What's the source of the derringer in *The Unvanquished?* I don't believe I have ever seen a derringer.

J. Faulkner: I don't know. I've seen some, but I don't have one. One night Brother Will gave me one of his rifles. I said, "But it's yours—you don't want to give me that," and he said, "Yes, take it home."

The table over yonder in the dining room is the one Brother Will describes in *The Unvanquished,* where Colonel Sartoris was telling his son Bayard that he was tired of killing, and he was twirling the wine glass, you know, and he said, "Tomorrow, when I go to town and meet Ben Redmond, I shall be unarmed."[59] That's the table he described.

S. Wolff: Was this the Old Colonel's table?

---

59. William Faulkner, *The Unvanquished* (New York, 1934), 266.

Fig. 12. The dining room table that belonged to William Clark Falkner, the Old Colonel. At a table such as this, Colonel Sartoris sat twirling a wineglass and planning to fight his last duel unarmed. (*Photograph by Billy Howard*)

J. Faulkner: Yes, it was. His son inherited it when he died.

S. Wolff: What kind of wood is it?

J. Faulkner: Burled oak. Quarter-sawing a log gives it this swirled effect.

F. Watkins: Where was the table when you got it?

J. Faulkner: Sue[60] had it—Uncle John's daughter, and it had come down through that side of the family. She said she wanted a new table, so I said, "I'll buy you a new table, and I'll take that one." So I did. Those two chairs were also the Old Colonel's. They were what he started his law practice in 1848 with.

F. Watkins: What is the type of bench in the entry hall with the lion's face and paws?

J. Faulkner: That was the Old Colonel's, too—1850, 1860. It used to have a mirror over it. Each armrest of the bench has a lion's face, and each front foot is shaped in the form of a lion's paw with a caster under it.

F. Watkins: [Points to shelf.] What about your books? Do you still have the $41,000 *Marionette* copy?

J. Faulkner: No, it was sold.

F. Watkins: What'd you get for it?

J. Faulkner: Thirty-something.

F. Watkins: You got all the first editions of William Faulkner's novels?

J. Faulkner: No, I don't think so. I'm missing one or two. Chooky[61] and I together have almost all of the first editions. Most of them are autographed by Brother Will to me; some are to me and Nan.[62] A few are simply signed by him.

F. Watkins: This is the first English edition of *The Sound and the Fury?*

J. Faulkner: Yes.

F. Watkins: Where do you keep your first editions?

60. Kathryn Sue Falkner.
61. Murry Cuthbert Falkner II, Jimmy's brother.
62. Nancy Jane Watson Faulkner, Jimmy's wife.

J. Faulkner: I keep them locked up.[63]

F. Watkins: I don't blame you.

J. Faulkner: Someone asked Brother Will which of his books he liked the best, and he said that a book is like a child; you can't favor one over another.

S. Wolff: Where did the walking sticks come from?

J. Faulkner: The Old Colonel brought back the big one from Mexico when he was fighting in the Mexican War in 1848. The other one, with *J. W. T. Falkner* on it, was the Young Colonel's walking stick, given to him by some people here in town. The other one with a sword in it was also his.

This was Brother Will's white cadet band. Cadets had to put this band around their caps to identify them as cadets instead of officers.

S. Wolff: This blank check is made out to you with his signature on it. When did he give this to you?

J. Faulkner: Brother Will used to keep a signed check with me all the time and said: "This is for anybody that might need it in the family. If anybody ever needs money, write the check and what the amount is, and I will replace it with another blank check." But also every time he needed anything done in Oxford, he would write or call me and say, "Go buy so and so and use that check, and I will have another one mailed to you today." So I would use the check, and he would send me another one. But this check is the last one he sent.[64]

S. Wolff: Is this ivory cigarette holder William Faulkner's?

J. Faulkner: Yes. That's the one he had stuck in his face one time in a fraternity picture of him. He had a part right in the middle of his head and swept his hair back. This is the same cigarette holder that is in that picture, I believe.

---

63. John Falkner notes that "Mother was proud of Bill's writings. . . . She always kept copies of [Bill's and my] books on a special table in the front room to show them off. Then she began missing them. . . . That's when Mother stopped keeping them where visitors could lay their hands on them. After that she moved my and Bill's books to a closet in her bedroom and them kept them locked up" (*my brother Bill,* 171).

64. See *ibid.,* 217–19.

S. Wolff: Do you know where it came from?

J. Faulkner: I have no idea. He had it a long time before I was born. These are his RAF wings, and this was Jack's letter opener.

S. Wolff: What kind of tobacco did he use?

J. Faulkner: Different kinds. I think he had one made in London.[65]

S. Wolff: When did he start smoking a pipe?

J. Faulkner: A good while before I was born.[66]

S. Wolff: Is Royal Air Force the same as Royal Canadian Air Force?

J. Faulkner: Yes and no. The Royal Canadian Air Force was in Canada, and its men were trained by the RAF. At a certain point in time, there was a switch over, and there was no more RCAF. It was just RAF. When the switch came, I don't know. Somebody argued with me for a long time about this switch. But there was a Royal Canadian Air Force at one time, and I think that's what he started out in.[67]

S. Wolff: Those are your flight wings?

J. Faulkner: Yes, I got them in Pensacola.

S. Wolff: Is this William Faulkner's watch—the one he had on when he died?

J. Faulkner: Yes. That silver one is the Old Colonel's, and he had it on when he was shot and killed in Ripley. That one is my great-grandfather's watch—the Young Colonel's; that one was Big Dad's. He was the first Murry C. Falkner—my grandfather.

65. William Faulkner claimed that his favorite tobacco was "blended for me by Dunhill in London when I was about nineteen, twenty years old; I've been smoking it ever since" (Meriwether and Millgate, eds., *Lion in the Garden,* 117). John Falkner points out that "Bill liked variety in his pipe tobacco. He would blend it differently at times to get a new taste and every time he would go into a pipe shop he'd buy several selections of ready-mixed tobacco. He would smoke from one can and then another, like a man trying different foods at each meal" (*my brother Bill,* 265).

66. See Blotner, who notes that Faulkner, as early as the fall of 1915, was a "pipe smoking youth" (Blotner, *Faulkner: A Biography* I, 177, 183). John Falkner notes that "Bill was a pipe smoker all his life" (*my brother Bill,* 264).

67. See Blotner, *Faulkner: A Biography,* I, 205–207, 210–33, for further details on Faulkner's war service in the Royal Air Force in Canada.

S. Wolff: Do the watches all still run?

J. Faulkner: Yes. They all still run.

S. Wolff: Is this Nanny's watch?

J. Faulkner: Yes.

S. Wolff: What is in this box?

J. Faulkner: That is Brother Will's navigator's box for his sailboat.[68] Here is the compass, and here is the martini flag that he raised every day at five o'clock.

He also used to have a wooden toolbox three feet long, two feet wide, and two feet high. It stayed on the back porch. He kept a lot of his papers in it. He used carpet tacks to put his initials on the top of the box.

S. Wolff: What happened to that box?

J. Faulkner: Jill took it back with her after the funeral, I think.

[Moving through the living room to the staircase in the hall.]

F. Watkins: Those your three children over there? [Points to portraits on the living room wall.]

J. Faulkner: Yes. I have three children.

S. Wolff: And you have a new grandchild whose name is William Faulkner?

J. Faulkner: Yes. Sure is. We call him Will.

S. Wolff: What is his full name?

J. Faulkner: William C. Faulkner. William Charles. We had a Murry Charles, rather than Murry Cuthbert, but still Murry C., and he still called himself "Jr." when he referred to himself as Murry C. Now, here, along the staircase are the pictures of the Faulkner men in the family, beginning at the top with the Old Colonel. [Points to the staircase on wall, upon which hang portraits of five generations of male Faulkner descendants.]

F. Watkins: I didn't recognize John, and [referring to a photograph of Jimmy Faulkner] that's you!

68. See Faulkner, *my brother Bill,* 233.

Fig. 13. A long line of Faulkners descends the staircase in the home of Jimmy Faulkner (*Photograph by Billy Howard*)

J. Faulkner: Yes. [Laughter.]

F. Watkins: That was a year or two ago, wasn't it?

J. Faulkner: Yes, it was; it sure was. Five or six. Hard years, too.

S. Wolff: When you look at this line of Faulkner portraits descending chronologically down the staircase, what do you feel?

J. Faulkner: You mean, do I feel intimidated?

S. Wolff: What do you feel?

J. Faulkner: I feel proud to be a part of the heritage. See what a strong resemblance there is in their eyes? All these eyes are alike—mostly brown and intense: two are blue, but just as intense.

S. Wolff: What do you discern of their personalities when you look at their eyes?[69]

J. Faulkner: The Old Colonel has eyes like a dozing lion. The power behind those eyes is something else. He has a piercing gaze, and it is focused on the future.

My double-second cousin, Sue Faulkner, a generation above me in relation to the Old Colonel, said that the Old Colonel would fight a buzz saw and give the buzz saw the first shot. He was the type of man who went for the jugular.

Now, the Young Colonel—his energy is more brooding and inward. He looks like he is about to explode.

People always underestimated Big Dad. When Big Dad died in '32, John stood in front of the bier and said, "Dad was a real man."[70]

John, my daddy, has eyes that were soft but intense, like waiting for an answer or an explanation. He could get mad, but he was very compassionate, just like Brother Will and Big Dad.

---

69. See *ibid.*, 220, for John Falkner's interpretation of the Faulkners' eyes.

70. *Cf.* Emma Jo Grimes Marshall's version of this story, told to her by Jimmy Faulkner: "Scenes from Yoknapatawpha: A Story of People and Places in the Real and Imaginary Worlds of William Faulkner" (Ph.D. dissertation, University of Alabama, 1978), 100.

The Chandler House

He wont hurt you. I pass here every day. He just runs along the fence.
—The Sound and the Fury

The Thompson-Chandler Mansion, or the Old Chandler House, as historians refer to it, was built around 1859 and owned by William Thompson, an Oxford attorney, planter, and brother to Jacob Thompson, the congressman and secretary of the interior under President Buchanan. The Chandler House was half-finished when the Civil War broke out, and Federal troops occupied it in 1862. Dr. Josiah Chandler moved into the house upon his marriage to Maria Lucretia, one of William Thompson's daughters. The fictional Compson home and family in The Sound and the Fury *bear a strong resemblance to the Chandler family and home, which have become emblematic of the fate of the postwar South and Faulkner's penchant for turning the "actual into apocryphal."* [71]

F. Watkins: This old and very large magnolia tree is all you can see from here. You almost can see more magnolia tree than you can house.

J. Faulkner: Yes. Now, this is the Old Chandler House [on the east side of a street running north and south just a block east of South Lamar]. That's what we call it. It's been sold. Notice, the fence is gone. Right along here there used to be a fence. A woman[72] had it taken down several years ago. She had it cut into pieces and shipped to Vicksburg. She sold it as the "Benjy Fence." There's one of the fence posts right here. The fence went around the house across the lawn and all the way down the front. Near the street corner right yonder, you can still see a stub of the fence sticking up.

F. Watkins: Does the house have two rooms on each floor? Four rooms and two hallways?

J. Faulkner: Right.

F. Watkins: Two large rooms on each floor? About how big are they?

71. Meriwether and Millgate, eds., *Lion in the Garden*, 255.
72. Irene Terry.

Fig. 14. The Chandler House, which bears a strong resemblance to the Compson home in *The Sound and the Fury* (*Courtesy Sally Wolff*)

J. Faulkner: About twenty by twenty. The same man must have designed this house, Brother Will's, and mine, because they're very similar.[73] The columns on this house are rectangular in shape like those at Brother Will's house. Mine are square.

S. Wolff: What is the ceiling height?

J. Faulkner: Probably twelve feet. Twelve feet downstairs, maybe, and ten feet upstairs.

S. Wolff: It's two stories, one room deep on each story, correct?

J. Faulkner: Yes, it was planned two rooms deep, but the war started, and everyone went off to war.

There were two houses being built—one on the next street, the Tate House—and the Chandler House. They had enough lumber to complete one house—the Tate—with some lumber left over. Dr. Chandler

73. Most likely William Turner, a contractor and architect who designed and built a large number of Oxford homes.

went off to war, and Mrs. Chandler borrowed the lumber and boarded up the back side of the Chandler House, which was not finished—just to get it enclosed. The original house had a cottage in the back. Later it was attached to the house and a kitchen was added to it. All this was torn down in the seventies.

A lot of times houses were built with the second floor only one room deep upstairs. Brother Will's is, on the west end.

S. Wolff: Was it common to add the kitchen later?

J. Faulkner: A lot of times they built a brick kitchen off away from the house to prevent fire in the big house. Most had a whistle walk: the slaves would whistle so the master would know they weren't eating the food.

Dr. Chandler was a surgeon in John Thompson's[74] cavalry. He was the father of Edwin Chandler, who was a prototype for the character Benjy Compson.[75] We will see the graves in the cemetery of Edwin's family: his brother, Wiley Chandler, and his sisters, Miss Annie Chandler Brown[76] and Miss Julia Chandler Logan.

Children used to walk to school this way and pass the Chandler House. They found out that when Edwin Chandler was out playing, they could irritate him to the point of near madness. His mother had to take him back inside when the children would come by from school everyday. That same event happens with Benjy.[77]

Edwin's mother asked her other children to promise they would never send him to a mental institution. So Wiley Chandler, Edwin's brother, stayed every night with him, and the two sisters took turns by staying in the daytime. I played with Edwin when my grandmother would bring me along on her visits to see his sisters. I had passed him mentally but not physically. Edwin was twenty years older than I, but his mind didn't go past six or seven years old.

74. Brother of Jacob Thompson.

75. See William Faulkner, *The Sound and the Fury;* Faulkner, *my brother Bill,* 271–73; Herman E. Taylor, *Faulkner's Oxford: Recollections and Reflections* (Nashville, 1990), 196; and Marshall, "Scenes from Yoknapatawpha," 217–19.

76. William Faulkner's first-grade teacher.

77. A similar account is recorded in Faulkner, *my brother Bill,* 271–73.

Back then, we didn't have natural gas, and we had coal in the fire-places. When everybody finished with *The Commercial Appeal,* Edwin would sit and tear it in strips, until he had a big pile in his lap. He was so good at the tearing that the paper looked like he cut it with a pair of scissors. The big event in his life was that he'd throw the whole pile of confetti in the air and holler "Wheee!" as it would come down like long snow.

He was sitting too near the fire one day when he threw the newspaper into the fire. It blew back out at him, burned, and killed him. I think it was that upstairs room on the right side.

F. Watkins: That could be a source for the paper dolls in *The Sound and the Fury.*

J. Faulkner: Could be.

F. Watkins: The short story "That Evening Sun" involves the Compson family—the same Compsons—and they are all little children, just as in *The Sound and the Fury,* but Nancy is another maid besides Dilsey. No stream, no golf course, nothing of that sort was associated with this house?

J. Faulkner: No, not that I know of.

F. Watkins: Is there a golf course around here that is supposedly like the golf course Faulkner creates?

J. Faulkner: Yes. The university golf course has moved twice that I know of. It used to be where the football and practice fields are now. It's moved now, though, north of the airport.

F. Watkins: So there's no story about a golf course ever being sold so that anybody could go to college?

J. Faulkner: Not that I know of.

F. Watkins: Nor that I do, either. Was Edwin Chandler castrated?

J. Faulkner: No, not that I know of.

F. Watkins: But as far as you know, he never raped anybody?

J. Faulkner: Oh, no, he never tried to, either.

F. Watkins: Now, the mother of Edwin Chandler, she wasn't a self-willed invalid like Mrs. Compson?

J. Faulkner: Not that I know of.

F. Watkins: Or a bad mother like that, in any sense?

J. Faulkner: No, no.

F. Watkins: Faulkner, as far as you know, created that out of his mind rather than taking it from a person?

J. Faulkner: Yes. Well, let's move along to town.

THE OXFORD JAIL

> So, although in a sense the jail was both older and less old than the courthouse, in actuality, in time, in observation and memory, it was older even than the town itself. . . . And so, being older than all, it had seen all . . . [To] peruse . . . the history of a community, look not in the church registers and the courthouse records, but beneath the successive layers of calsomine and creosote and whitewash on the walls of the jail, since only in that forcible carceration does man find the idleness in which to compose . . . the gross and simple recapitulations of his gross and simple heart.
>
> —*Requiem for a Nun*

In Requiem for a Nun, *Faulkner describes the jail as older even than the town of Jefferson. For him the jail, like the cemetery, measures the history of a community. Faulkner saw a profound significance in the building of a jail as the inaugural act of a community: through it the community might control evil, violence, and crime before turning its attentions and energies to nobler human achievements. A jail stands as a monument to the history of a community and, as Faulkner indicates, a crucible for realizing and (perhaps) changing the soul.*

[In downtown Oxford, near the new jail, which was built on the site of the old jail.]

J. Faulkner: Now, the jail is up this street, North Lamar.

F. Watkins: It is a pity that we can't see the old jail. It began as a log house and then had brick and weather boarding. How many layers were there?

J. Faulkner: Oh, I don't know. The first time I remember it, it was just red brick.

F. Watkins: But that was on the outside with logs on the inside.

J. Faulkner: When I knew it, it was all brick.

F. Watkins: Is there any story about the beginning of the Oxford Jail like Faulkner tells in *Requiem for a Nun*—having a bunch of outlaws and making a place to put them?

J. Faulkner: Not that I know of.

F. Watkins: Sanctuary has a jail modeled on the old one. Joe Christmas broke out of one like it, and Mink Snopes was put into a similar one. The old jail was the only jail until this concrete building you see up here, which was put here in the last twenty years.

Jimmy, do you know what a heaven tree is?[78]

J. Faulkner: No.

F. Watkins: We don't have them; I think they're what we call cottonwoods in Georgia.

J. Faulkner: Now, that could very well be. In his fiction Brother Will talked about a heaven tree in the corner of the jail yard.

F. Watkins: I remember seeing it when it was called a heaven tree in 1957.

J. Faulkner: [Beside the Holiday Inn on the corner of Jefferson Avenue and North Lamar in Oxford.] From where we stand now, we can look to the south about four blocks and see the Lafayette County Courthouse that was in some of Brother Will's stories. Then two blocks south of us, about halfway between here and the courthouse—where that modern, out-of-place, ugly building on the east side of the street stands—is the new Oxford jail.

F. Watkins: They replace the best with the worst.

J. Faulkner: Yes. That is where the old, two-story, red-brick jail stood during the 1800s and the first half of the 1900s. That was where Nelse Patton was a trusty in jail. A trusty was a convict that was trusted by the sheriff to run errands out in town and then come back at a certain time.

78. A possible reference to the *Ailanthus altissima,* a popular species of tree planted in large cities to provide shade. Known also as the "tree of heaven," the *A. altissima* flourishes in the South, although it is not usually found in northern Mississippi. See "*Ailanthus altissima,*" *Collier's Enclyclopedia* (New York, 1993), 308. William Faulkner describes this tree in front of the jail in his fiction. See John B. Cullen, with Floyd C. Watkins, *Old Times in the Faulkner Country* (Baton Rouge, 1975), 65–66, and Pilkington, *Stark Young,* 77, which discusses Stark Young's work *Heaven Trees.*

One time in 1907, when Brother Will was about ten years old, a white man named McMillan[79] was put in jail for being drunk. At the time Oxford didn't have electricity or telephones, so Mr. McMillan asked Nelse Patton to go to his house about two miles north and tell his wife, Mrs. McMillan, where he was. Nelse Patton did go to the McMillan home and went in the front door. This was not done back then. He thought Mrs. McMillan was alone, so he accosted her. Her daughter was there, and they both screamed and ran outside to the front yard. Patton caught Mrs. McMillan and cut her throat with a straight razor. During the autopsy, Dr. Young, the father of Stark Young, found a broken piece of metal embedded in Mrs. McMillan's spine that matched and fit the missing piece of Patton's razor.

Nelse Patton ran and wound up in a big ditch that is a block west of where we are. He went west along this ditch, the same as Joe Christmas did in *Light in August*. The ditch led him to Toby Tubby Creek, west of town, where he was caught and brought back to jail, the same as Joe Christmas.

That night, about dark, a crowd began to gather in front of the jail, and former senator Sullivan,[80] who lived about two blocks north of where we are now, went to the jail and made a fiery speech to the crowd, turning it into an uncontrolled mob. He told them to break into the jail and kill Nelse Patton because of what he had done to a white woman. Here, again, the reason for the attack on Joe Christmas was similar.

My mother, who was about five years old at that time and who lived about two blocks east of the jail, told me that she could hear the men pecking and chipping at the brick wall outside Patton's cell until they finally broke in. I remember the newer, light-colored brick used to patch up the hole in the wall where the men crawled through to get to Nelse Patton. Patton only had a wooden stool to defend himself with. He fought off the men for a while but was finally overcome and killed. His

79. See Cullen and Watkins, *Old Times*, 89–98, for a similar account of the story. According to Cullen, the name *McMillan* had several spellings.

80. On former United States senator W. V. Sullivan's role in the Nelse Patton incident, see Cullen and Watkins, *Old Times*, 91, 97–98.

Fig. 15. Through this overhanging trail, known around Oxford as the Big Ditch, Nelse Patton ran after the murder of a townswoman. Faulkner depicts the story and the ditch in *Light in August*. (*Photograph by Billy Howard*)

body was mutilated, and he was taken to the courthouse yard and hung from a tree. My mother's older sister[81] told me that her mother took her to town the next day but made her walk on the inside of her, next to the stores, so she wouldn't have to look at Nelse Patton's hanging body.

81. Marvel Ramey Sisk.

This must have made a real lasting impression on Brother Will, because so much of it is in *Light in August.*

F. Watkins: When did this happen?

J. Faulkner: 1908. Brother Will was ten years old then.

F. Watkins: Now, as we use our imaginations, when we go to the cemetery by way of the courthouse, we remember Benjy—the character whose house, the Chandler House, was the model for *The Sound and the Fury*—his great avocation was coming to the cemetery. He would come around the square, turn right, and go to the cemetery. That was his pattern. Benjy came around that square and went to the cemetery. When, at the end of *The Sound and the Fury,* Luster turned around to go the wrong way around the square, that made the world come backwards to Benjy. That was too much for Benjy's mind.

J. Faulkner: We can look to the east about five blocks to the cemetery where our family is buried.

F. Watkins: Here's the ditch where Nelse Patton ran through to escape. I thought the town was going to fill in this ditch, Jimmy.

J. Faulkner: Fill it full? They did begin in the 1980s to fill in part of it. You can take pictures, but, of course, a color picture of Joe Christmas' ditch just doesn't seem right. It should be black and white.

F. Watkins: In the wintertime. Where might be a model for Hightower's house?

J. Faulkner: I have always pictured Dr. Frank Moody Purser's house as the model for Hightower's house. It is down east of the square on Jackson Street, near the courthouse. Dr. Purser was a Baptist preacher, and he may have been the model for Hightower. Also a Hightower family lives out east of Abbeville.

Hightower's wife committed suicide, and so did Dr. Purser's wife, but she drank Lysol. He was going around with another woman, the woman he married next, at the time it happened. Dr. Purser lived in the Tyler Avenue and Fifth Street house after his second marriage.

F. Watkins: How do you figure out that this is like the big ditch that Joe Christmas ran through?

J. Faulkner: See, the ditch runs from the jail up yonder. This was the big ditch that came down through by the jail. That's where Patton broke away and ran by the jail and down the ditch. It turns around and comes down to Toby Tubby Creek. That's where, in the novel, they caught Joe Christmas.

University of Mississippi Reading Room

Townspeople taking after-supper drives through the college grounds or an oblivious and bemused faculty member or a candidate for a master's degree on his way to the library would see Temple, a snatched coat under her arm and her long legs blonde with running, in speeding silhouette against the lighted windows of the Coop, as the women's dormitory was known, vanishing into the shadow beside the library wall . . .

—*Sanctuary*

The University of Mississippi—repository for, among other things, some of Faulkner's manuscripts—appears in several of Faulkner's works, including The Unvanquished *and* Sartoris. *The Coop, a woman's dormitory on the Ole Miss campus, appears in* Sanctuary. *In this section Jimmy Faulkner recounts stories of Faulkner's Hollywood days, his opposition to big government, and his distinctive style.*

[On the Ole Miss campus.]

J. Faulkner: Look at the steeple on the right, on top of the old law building, which later became the geology building. They were going to get someone to paint it a long time ago when Brother Will volunteered to paint it. Nanny found out about it, and she and Brother Will had a confrontation about the painting of the steeple. Brother Will said he was going to do it, and Nanny said, "You're not." It finally came to a compromise: Brother Will could paint it if he just wouldn't tell her when he was going to do it.[82]

S. Wolff: He did paint it, didn't he?

J. Faulkner: Yes.

82. John Falkner implies that Nanny did not know about the job until its completion: "They were painting the law building, which had a steeple. No one else would paint the steeple so Bill did. He tied himself to it with ropes and painted it from top to bottom. After that Mother told Dad not to get Bill any more jobs without talking it over with her first" (*Cf.* Faulkner, *my brother Bill,* 142, and Marshall, "Scenes from Yoknapatawpha," 146).

S. Wolff: What year was that?

J. Faulkner: I'd guess in the mid-1920s.

Now, this is the library. On the building right there is a quotation from the Nobel Prize speech: "I decline to accept the end of man. . . . I believe that man will not merely endure: he will prevail."

[Entering the Mississippi Reading Room, where Faulkner's books and manuscripts are on display.]

S. Wolff: William Faulkner wrote the script for the movie *Stallion Road,* didn't he?

J. Faulkner: Yes. Someone once asked him who the main character was, and he said, "The horse." [Laughter.] Somebody also wrote him and said he didn't like the movie; Brother Will wrote back and said, "My horse didn't like it, either." [Laughter.]

S. Wolff: Ronald Reagan was in that movie, wasn't he?

J. Faulkner: Yes. Steve McQueen was in *The Reivers.* When they were filming *To Have and Have Not,* Howard Hawks, the director, bet somebody that he could take the worst thing that Hemingway ever did and make a top movie out of it. They got Brother Will to write the script, and it was top. He was writing as they were shooting the film, and he wrote one sentence that was pages long for Humphrey Bogart to say. Humphrey Bogart looked at him, started laughing, and said, "Hell, I can't memorize that." [Laughter.] So they had to break it down into two sentences that Bogart could memorize.

J. Faulkner: [Describing a sample of William Faulkner's handwriting on display in a showcase on the back wall of the room.] Brother Will liked to draw a line down the left side of the page to create a two-inch margin so that he could make his corrections. Most people write 250 words on a page. He could get over 1,200. He wrote small.[83]

S. Wolff: Twelve hundred words to a page!

J. Faulkner: The other scriptwriters in Hollywood would turn out maybe eight pages a day. He'd turn out forty. They got mad at him. They

---

83. John Falkner's version is that William Faulkner wrote so small because he said "he had only so many miles of ink left and he aimed to make as many words out of them as he could" (*my brother Bill,* 161, 244).

said, "The union just doesn't like that." He said, "I'm not in the union." He didn't believe in any organizations, really. He also said most critics were failed writers, anyway. [Laughter.]

S. Wolff: Was William Faulkner opposed to unions?

J. Faulkner: He said a man will get hold of a union and use it for his own self-aggrandizement.[84] He was independent. He didn't join anything. He believed a man should stand or fall on his own two feet. But he did join the RAF, the SAE,[85] and the Quiet Birdmen, a pilot's organization.

S. Wolff: What were some of William Faulkner's other interests?

J. Faulkner: He loved track. He was refereeing one time at a track meet at the University of Virginia, and they sent word down to tell him that there was a check in the bursar's office for him. They asked him to come out and pick it up. So he went by to get it, and they said they wanted his Social Security number, and he said, "I don't have one." They said, "We can't give you a check without your Social Security number," and he said, "I'd rather not have a check." So he was never paid for it.

S. Wolff: That illustrates his objection to governmental interference in private affairs.

J. Faulkner: That's right.

S. Wolff: Did William Faulkner have a Social Security number?

J. Faulkner: No. Certain categories of people then didn't have to have one. He didn't have a Social Security number because he was self-employed.

Another time he was on his houseboat, the *Minmagary*. Two doctor brothers lived down the road from him, Felix and Dewey Linder. Dewey was a dentist, and Felix was a general practitioner. They were the same age as Brother Will. They'd gone to school together, and they knew he wouldn't have a radio or a television set in his house.

84. John Falkner comments that William Faulkner did contribute once to the Communist party in support of a Communist party member living in Lafayette County: "It was simply Bill's tribute to a man standing" for his own individuality (*ibid.*, 226–28).

85. Sigma Alpha Epsilon. See Blotner, *Faulkner: A Biography,* I, 254–57, and Faulkner, *my brother Bill,* 143, for further details.

They were going out on the houseboat one afternoon, and Dewey brought a battery-operated radio along. They got on the boat, and Dewey said, "Bill, President Truman is going to make a speech this afternoon; I'd like to hear it." Dewey didn't cut the radio on until time for the speech. Brother Will sat down to listen to it, because he was a perfect host. When Truman got through with his speech—the theme was "we're going to give this, and we're going to give that"—Brother Will said, "Well, we've got a wonderful country, but we can't afford it." [86]

He was antigovernment, especially the IRS. [Laughter.] He was coming back from some State Department trip, and I flew up to Memphis to pick him up. I landed on a little airstrip on Mud Island, just off the end of Union Avenue. I would always meet him in the Peabody, the famous old hotel in Memphis. I told him I had an airplane and said, "Brother Will, you put your bag in the airplane, and I'll go over and pay the landing fee." He said, "No, I'll pay it. I'll write a check for it." I said, "It's just a dollar and a half." He said, "I can take it off my income tax. I believe that it is my duty as a private citizen to beat the government out of every penny I possibly can." [87] He wrote a check for a dollar and a half!

S. Wolff: Did he watch the films for which he had written scripts?

J. Faulkner: He went to watch *Intruder in the Dust* because his mother wanted to see it. He was not going to the reception when they got through making *Intruder in the Dust,* and Aunt 'Bama[88] found out about it. She called him and said, "Billy, I'm coming, and you are going to take me to the reception and the premiere." He said, "Yes, ma'am." That's how come he went.[89]

I don't think he really saw the movies he wrote for. He felt the same way about his books. He said once that when the first person buys the first book, it was no longer his.[90]

86. *Cf.* Marshall, "Scenes from Yoknapatawpha," 307.

87. When asked by a representative of the Bureau of Internal Revenue what he did with his money, Faulkner snapped, "None of your damn business" (Blotner, *Faulkner: A Biography,* II, 1682). See also Marshall, "Scenes from Yoknapatawpha," 307.

88. Alabama Leroy Falkner, the Old Colonel's youngest daughter by his second wife.

89. See Blotner, *Faulkner: A Biography,* II, 1296–97, and Minter, *William Faulkner,* 215, for corroboration.

90. See Faulkner, *my brother Bill,* 242.

S. Wolff: Another distinctive feature of his handwriting is the way he made his s's and n's.

J. Faulkner: The n's—when you print them with a little too much space between the parts of the letter, will come out like he wrote them, like that [𝗻]. An s—now, I don't know about that. That looks like a 2 to me.

I'll tell you what my daddy said at one time. They said everybody tries to read all these things into his works, and there is nothing hidden in his works, but he was a damn good storyteller. I think the way he felt about everything comes out in the Nobel Prize speech and that graduation speech.

S. Wolff: He allowed Estelle to read his manuscripts before they were published, didn't he?

J. Faulkner: I never saw her read them, but at times he would read passages to her. I think his mother read them. If we happened to be down at his house, he would read it to himself—out in the side yard. I've heard him do that.[91]

91. John Falkner said that whenever William Faulkner wrote a flying story, he invited John into his room to read it (*ibid.,* 155). Minter also points out that "Faulkner spent hours talking and reading poetry to Estelle's daughter, Victoria" (Minter, *William Faulkner,* 175).

2

LAFAYETTE COUNTY CHURCHES AND CEMETERIES

My idea is, a tombstone in a public cemetery is set up as a true part of the record of a community.

—William Faulkner to Jim Faulkner,
[probably May or June, 1961],
Selected Letters of William Faulkner

Jimmy Faulkner points out several churches and cemeteries in and around Oxford. Each location visited is steeped in local history, folklore, and legend. William Faulkner believed that the cemetery is a distinct part of the history of a community; the gravestones, epitaphs, and dates are often the only visible traces of human lives. Here are names, either exact or barely altered, recognizable in Faulkner's fiction. Others are merely suggestive of fictional counterparts. These dead speak now, as they spoke to Faulkner, of the Civil War and subsequent freedom; of other pasts, other histories, and other relationships within communities now silent, but not entirely forgotten.

The first stop is the Toby Tubby Church Cemetery, named, along with the creek nearby, for the famed Chickasaw chief who once lived in the area.[1] *Today, all that remains of the church and its cemetery are a few stones, testaments to the era of the Civil War. Most of the interred bear the surnames of their white masters. Few grave markers show date of birth—those dates were unknown or unrecorded—only the date of death appears. Other graves are completely unmarked. Those graves that are inscribed show that the interred were born in slavery and died after the Civil War. Here, among the tombstones, the conversation focuses upon funeral practices in the South and particularly in Oxford; folklore, voodoo, and the survival, until recently, of the use of tribal drums as a form of communication in the black community.*

Jimmy Faulkner next details the history of College Hill Church and Cemetery as the site where William and Estelle Faulkner married. The marriage of Thomas Sutpen and Ellen Coldfield occurs in a church modeled upon this one in Absalom, Absalom! *Behind the church, beyond a barbed-wire fence and brambles, are the graves of slaves, now six-foot oblong depressions in the earth, names lost to time and dust.*

The last stop is St. Peter's, Oxford's largest cemetery, which is redolent of community history and of the Faulkner family in particular. Jimmy Faulkner points out the graves of townspeople and relatives who, in life, provided William Faulkner with models for his characters. Some Jimmy knew personally. Inevitably, he begins to recount tall tales about friends awaking drunk in the cemetery, stories about the Civil War, and a yarn about Mammy Callie's last trip to Arkansas. A walk through the Faulkner burial ground and to the grave of William Faulkner himself elicits stories about Faulkner and his family, his religious beliefs, and the artist's awareness that the names on these tombstones are more than just the legends of forgotten dreams; they identify lives, community, and home.

Toby Tubby Church Cemetery

J. Faulkner: The church building itself has rotted and is no longer here, but the cemetery is still here. Most of the people buried here were

---

1. Blotner states that Toby Tubby was "the old Chickasaw chief who was a wealthy slave owner when Ishtehotopah signed the Treaty of Pontotoc." Legend has it that his daughter dug into his burial mound after his death in search of government money that supposedly had been buried with him (Blotner, *Faulkner: A Biography,* I, 72–73). See Beverly Young Langford, "History and Legend in William Faulkner's 'Red Leaves,'" *Notes on Mississippi Writers,* VI (1972), 21–22, for a discussion of the spellings of the name "Toby Tubby." The Toby Tubby Creek crosses the northwest corner of Lafayette County.

slaves, but some are more recently deceased. The cemetery is still in active use. The names on these gravestones—Lewis, Wilson, and Pettis—are names of some of the white men the people buried here worked for. The slaves originally took the names of their masters; then, after the Civil War, many kept these last names.

As slaves, they went to their masters' churches. When they were freed, their former masters welcomed them to come to church, but they wanted a church of their own. White people contributed what they could to help them. Mostly these churches were wood frames. That's how Toby Tubby was built.

Some of their graves do have stones. Before the war they couldn't have headstones; after they were freed, they could.

S. Wolff: This man's name was Toby Turner. Toby is a frequent name around town, isn't it?

J. Faulkner: Yes. Few of these stones have birth dates. Most of these people did not know when they were born, and most in this cemetery died in the 1870s and 1880s.

S. Wolff: They were born in slavery and died in freedom.

J. Faulkner: They turned to the church for hope.

S. Wolff: Here on these tombstones are names that are familiar in William Faulkner's stories: Doc, Hightower, Millie, Cora, Buford, Moses, H[o]uston.[2] The inscriptions also offer comforting thoughts: "In Heaven there is one angel more"; "We will meet"; "It's alright"; "O death where is thy sting / O grave where is thy victory"; "Asleep in Jesus."

Look at this one: Nancy Herrod. Her stone lists no birth date, only the date she died, 1906. "Aged 54 years." At least this stone says her age. Most do not. Here's another woman born in slavery: "Jane / Wife of Lewis Johnson. D. January 11, 1900. Age 65 / Honored, Beloved, and Wife / Here Mother Lies."

J. Faulkner: Buford was the first white family to settle here.

2. See Frances Willard Pate, "Names of Characters in Faulkner's Mississippi" (Ph.D. dissertation, Emory University, 1969); and Elmo Howell, "William Faulkner's Graveyard," *Notes on Mississippi Writers,* IV (1972), 115–18.

S. Wolff: Tell us about the funeral customs of black people in your area.

J. Faulkner: The blacks who were on our place, or real close to us through the years, would go with our family to a family funeral, and I would go to the black funerals I felt we should be represented at: Renzi, Uncle Ned, Pearlie, and Nat.[3] Sometimes Nan, my wife, went. We would try to get there in time for the lowering of the casket. We would leave after the body was buried, and they would continue with the funeral. Whenever a friend of mine in the black community died, I took my children to the funeral.

In the black community here, the custom is to open the coffin to take pictures. Until recently, the oldest white member of the family would then put the first shovel of dirt on the blacks' graves. Black people would let us do this and lead the funeral service. This custom began in the slave days. Sometimes people in both the black and white community dug their own graves before they died to save the money it would cost later. All the burial would then cost was the price of the box.

F. Watkins: When Mr. Compson is buried in *The Sound and the Fury,* Uncle Bascomb throws dirt in the grave. Pall bearers used to wear white gloves and throw them in the grave after they had gotten rid of the coffin, after they had deposited the casket.[4]

J. Faulkner: What we do is take a boutonniere—a rose—and put it on the casket. I don't know about the gloves.

F. Watkins: Well, now, I wonder if it wasn't associated with corpses or diseases?

J. Faulkner: Probably so. Black funerals go on a long time here. Renzi was a black man on our place; he died in the late sixties. His fu-

---

3. Lorenzo (also Arenza, Renzi, or Rinsy) McJunkin was a driver and farm worker for William Faulkner. See Blotner, *Faulkner: A Biography,* II, 1089, and Cullen and Watkins, *Old Times,* 50–51. Ned Barnett ("Uncle Ned"), a former slave belonging to the Old Colonel, worked for William and Estelle Faulkner as yard man and butler. See Blotner, *Faulkner: A Biography,* I, 658, and Faulkner, *my brother Bill,* 182–86, for further details. Pearlie was the wife of Jimmy's workman, Joby, a former convict whose responsibilities included working Jimmy's land and caring for Jimmy's children. Nat Avant was the wife of James Avant.
4. See Faulkner, *The Sound and the Fury,* for details.

neral was an all-day affair. They start in the morning, and they bury in the afternoon. I was the only white person there. They asked me to sit with the family. They had two or three preachers, picnics, and so forth. The body was buried before dark.

S. Wolff: Do all the festivities occur before the burial?

J. Faulkner: Yes.

S. Wolff: What other customs do you recall?

J. Faulkner: When Big Dad died in 1932, there were few phones in Oxford. Usually when somebody died, the white family would write an invitation out. A colored man would put it on a silver platter and go door to door inviting people to the funeral by having them read the invitation.[5] Big Dad was the last person we did this for. We asked Uncle Ned to walk around with a silver tray, and the white folks read the announcement card on the tray that Big Dad had died and where the funeral was. Brother Will was in California at the time.

F. Watkins: I never did get any explanation for the totemlike figures I saw in a man's yard near here some years back. Do you remember it?

J. Faulkner: I remember seeing it. If I'm not mistaken, it's up east of Abbeville.

F. Watkins: Yes. That was a long time ago. You have no idea whether it's there or not?

J. Faulkner: No, I sure don't.

F. Watkins: Tell about the drums, Jimmy.

J. Faulkner: The drums just stopped about ten years ago, maybe fifteen [1965–70], but until then black people still talked to each other on drums at night. We'd sit outside on summer nights and listen to them, and drums would start beating on one side of the Toby Tubby Creek. Then the drums back here in Tallahatchie Bottom would start answering, and they'd talk all night.

Joby and Pearlie, a couple then living on my place, acted like they were hypnotized by the drums. They believed they were voodooed together by a spell. They also thought that if they were ever to separate, they would need to have someone with that same power to unvoodoo

---

5. *Cf.* the wedding of Thomas Sutpen and Ellen Coldfield in *Absalom, Absalom!*

them. They did not believe they could simply get a divorce. Joby's sister did have this power to break the voodoo spell, but she wouldn't do it because she liked Pearlie.

The drums had a special power too, I guess. People would hear them, get up, and walk straight as a plumb line to those drums, through barbed-wire fences, briar thickets, anything—to the source of the drum beat. They were hypnotized by it; they'd be gone all night long.

F. Watkins: You have heard that and seen that yourself?

J. Faulkner: Yes.

F. Watkins: Ten years ago?

J. Faulkner: Ten, twelve years ago—maybe a little longer.

F. Watkins: Did you ever follow them?

J. Faulkner: Wouldn't have gone there for anything in the world.

F. Watkins: The survival in modern times is unbelievable.

J. Faulkner: I've never heard anything like that, have you? They just talked to each other on them. The old ones did it. They got telephones out here now, I guess.

F. Watkins: That's the most disappointing thing I've heard you say. [Laughter.]

J. Faulkner: That's the only thing that made it stop, I guess.

S. Wolff: Did William Faulkner ever hear the drums?

J. Faulkner: Lord, yes. When the drums got the air vibrating, you could hear them for miles.[6]

F. Watkins: You know how William Faulkner hated telephones; I'll bet he would have liked the drums better.

J. Faulkner: Oh, yes.

COLLEGE HILL CHURCH

J. Faulkner: This is College Hill Presbyterian Church, established in 1836. This was the first building in the community; then they built Miss Pearle's store. The church bricks were made by slave labor. The

---

6. See Blotner, *Faulkner: A Biography,* II, 1776, for confirmation.

Fig. 16. Inside the College Hill Presbyterian Church, where
William and Estelle Faulkner were married and upon which
Faulkner modeled the church in *Absalom, Absalom!*
(*Photograph by Billy Howard*)

people who lived here had slaves. Many of the blacks here have names of
the people who were the early settlers. The slaves were also communing
members of the church.

F. *Watkins:* They were in many other white communities, too.

J. *Faulkner:* Two or three hundred Ole Miss students come out
here weekly to church during the regular terms every year.

[In the sanctuary, Jimmy points to the back wall of the church opposite
the pulpit.]

J. *Faulkner:* You can see—they've sort of filled them in now—but
there were two stoves. Right in here, where the pews are, there was an
open place. That's where they had their stoves for heat in the wintertime.
There was also a slave balcony that was torn down years and years ago.
Nobody here even remembers it. But you can see from the outside the
brick that filled in the doors up there. Those doors opened to the outside
from the balcony.

The town was established in 1835. Most of the people here migrated from a little town close to Columbia, Tennessee. They had a split in the church up there, and this half moved down here. Presbyterians used to own all the land out here until taxes took some of it in 1866 and 1867. They just wouldn't sell any; you couldn't get it.

This was—and still is—the center of activities for most of the folks around here. The school was chartered shortly after College Hill had begun settling.

F. Watkins: The church ceiling certainly is modern lumber, isn't it?

J. Faulkner: That's a beaded ceiling.

F. Watkins: Does that mean modern or old?

J. Faulkner: It's an old style, which was common at the turn of the century. Let's say you have a one-inch-by-four-inch board. Grooves are cut along the length of the middle section of the board for decoration. These boards also have a tongue-and-groove structure that fits them together side by side. We have beaded ceilings in my house and my mother's in Oxford.

F. Watkins: So this plaster was also partly plastered by slaves. Are slaves and whites buried together back behind the church?

J. Faulkner: No, they're not buried together. There's a fence separating the graves, and no markers on slaves' graves.

F. Watkins: Rocks?

J. Faulkner: No. The graves are unmarked.

S. Wolff: Let's walk around to the back of the church to the cemetery.

J. Faulkner: Now, here's the tombstone with the name of Bunch, like Byron Bunch in *Light in August.*

S. Wolff: Where are the slave graves?

J. Faulkner: Back there, behind this cemetery and through that barbed-wire fence.

S. Wolff: I see rows of oval-shaped indentations, sunken, at least two feet down in the earth and partially covered with brambles.

J. Faulkner: These graves sank, but you can see the indentations going back about fifty feet over that way.

S. Wolff: They number twenty or so. No markers exist.

Fig. 17. A tombstone in the slave section of the College Hill Church Cemetery (*Photograph by Billy Howard*)

Fig. 18. Amid the brambles are the sunken, unmarked graves of slaves buried behind the College Hill Presbyterian Church. (*Photograph by Billy Howard*)

St. Peter's Cemetery

This cemetery is cooled by large, spreading cedars, offering shade against the heat bearing down upon grave-side visitors in the humid Mississippi July afternoon. A walk through the cemetery provokes reminiscences about certain people, their roles in William Faulkner's life, and their immortalization in his art.

J. Faulkner: Floyd, this is Auntee[7] buried right here. You know Granny Millard in *The Unvanquished?*

F. Watkins: Yes.

J. Faulkner: Auntee and Granny Millard were alike in character—both strong women.

F. Watkins: Was someone actually killed by a bushwhacker?

J. Faulkner: Yes. I think it was in south Mississippi, not in Oxford, not in my family. This is Sallie,[8] you know, the little girl who played with John, Jack,[9] and Brother Will?

F. Watkins: Right, Sallie Murry.

J. Faulkner: I'm going to see if I can find L. Q. C. Lamar's[10] grave for you. Jacob Thompson gave this land, the original land, for the cemetery. After the war he was wiped out; he went to Memphis, but he was never the same after that. But he gave L. Q. C. Lamar a grave site. He said, "I know you're not going to have any money, so I'm going to give you a place so you can be buried." Jacob Thompson gave L. Q. C.

7. Mary Holland Falkner Wilkins, William Faulkner's paternal aunt.

8. Sallie Murry Wilkins, daughter of Mary Holland Faulkner and Dr. J. Porter Wilkins, and first cousin of William Faulkner, with whom she spent many childhood hours.

9. Murry "Jack" Charles Falkner, Jr., William Faulkner's brother. Jack joined the FBI in 1925, resigned three years later, and applied for reinstatement in 1933. With the outbreak of World War II, he left the FBI to serve in the army's Counter Intelligence Corps. Jack rejoined the FBI in 1946. See Murry C. Falkner, *The Falkners of Mississippi: A Memoir* (Baton Rouge, 1967), 120–23, 169–70, 185.

10. Lucius Quintus Cincinnatus Lamar, associate justice of the United States Supreme Court (1888–91), helped draft Mississippi's Secession Ordinance of 1861. See "Lamar, Lucius Quintus Cincinnatus," in *The Encyclopedia of Southern History*, ed. David C. Roller and Robert W. Twyman (Baton Rouge, 1979), 704.

Fig. 19. The Faulkner family plots in St. Peter's Cemetery
(*Photograph by Billy Howard*)

Lamar that grave site. Floyd, here's Jacob Thompson right here: 1838–1897. Now, here you are, right here is Edwin Chandler.

F. Watkins: This is the grave of the one who served as the proto-type for Benjy Compson in *The Sound and the Fury?*

J. Faulkner: Yes. I used to play with him. I liked him.

F. Watkins: What age was he mentally?

J. Faulkner: Six or seven.

F. Watkins: Faulkner portrayed Benjy as even less able mentally.

J. Faulkner: Yes.

F. Watkins: He would run along the fence?

J. Faulkner: Yes. Oh, he was a good baseball player: knock a ball a country mile. He would play with John, Brother Will, and everybody.

F. Watkins: He was fifty-five when he died?

J. Faulkner: Yes.

F. Watkins: Aren't there several pictures in town of initials or names scratched on a window pane?[11]

J. Faulkner: One that I know of. There's one in my house. When they took the pane out and repaired it, they turned it upside down.

F. Watkins: [Reading from tombstone.] Look at this inscription: "He sits by the side of his wife of whom he never thought himself worthy." I don't believe any couple in the world is in that condition. "In every innocent moment of his life, she went hand in hand and heart with him for over fifty-one years." What about all the guilty moments of his life? Oh, look! "The above epitaph was written by his own hand a short time before his death."

J. Faulkner: What's the last line?

F. Watkins: "He leaves behind him a memory as beloved as it was honored." Now, where's L. Q. C.?

J. Faulkner: Here. He had a lot to do with writing the Confederate constitution, and after the war he became a Supreme Court justice, showing that he was well respected around the country, and not just in the South. You can see Lamar's grave right in here.

J. Faulkner: That's the Oldhamses'.

F. Watkins: Look at these old cedars. [Turning to look at the Thompson burial place.] Can you see the similarity between the names of Jacob Thompson and Jason Compson? Faulkner changed the letters to create a new name.

J. Faulkner: Yes.

S. Wolff: Can you suggest who might have inspired the portrait of the unscrupulous Flem Snopes?

J. Faulkner: Well, there are certain individuals in Oxford who carried on the activities of Flem Snopes almost exactly, but I will not name them here.

Now, here is the tombstone for Mr. Culley Archibald. He passed out from drinking one day around five o'clock P.M. while in a furniture

---

11. *Cf.* William Faulkner, *Requiem for a Nun* (New York, 1951), 229, in which a girl stands at her window, sees a soldier go by, and scratches a face on the window pane. When the soldier returns, he marries her.

store that sold baby cribs and coffins. For a joke his friends laid him out in a coffin—really laid him out, you know, with his hands crossed over his chest. But his friend, Mr. Claude Roach, said, "I'd better stay in here with him so he won't go completely crazy when he comes to."

When he came to, he asked, "Where am I?" Mr. Claude said, "You've died and come to hell." Mr. Culley said, "Well, how long have you been here?" Mr. Claude said, "Three hundred years," and Mr. Culley replied, "Then you must know where we can get a drink!"

S. Wolff: That's a good story to tell in the cemetery.

J. Faulkner: Sure is. Now, here is the highest monument in the cemetery. It's Grandfather's. He had a bet with Mr. Bem Price[12] that the one who lived the longest could build the highest monument.[13] Grandfather beat him, and his monument is six inches taller.

S. Wolff: Here is Joella Pegues Shegog: 1839 to 1928. Is this family name related to that of the Shegogs who built Rowan Oak and like the name of the Reverend Shegog of *The Sound and The Fury?*[14]

J. Faulkner: Yes. Now, here is Buster Crouch. He was a drinking buddy of Brother Will's. He was a big man and had a bigger hat size than Brother Will. After they had been drinking a while, they would switch hats. Later, you could see Brother Will walking home with that big hat on, and you would know that he had a hangover.

One day, when John and Jack passed him on the sidewalk on the way to school—he was coming home with that big hat sitting on his head and coming down over his eyes like Laurel of "Laurel and Hardy"—John said, "Mornin' Bill." Brother Will just kept walking with the hat drawn way down over his eyes and said, "Goddamn it."[15]

Now, here is the stone of Marvin Hawkins, who might be a good source for Pat Stamper.[16] He was a horse trader.

---

12. Cashier of the Bank of Oxford, influential Oxford businessman, and Faulkner family friend.

13. See Blotner, *Faulkner: A Biography,* I, 335–36, for corroboration.

14. See *ibid.,* 651–52.

15. See a corroborating story by John Cullen in Cullen and Watkins, *Old Times,* 52.

16. See William Faulkner, *The Hamlet* (New York, 1940). During the Pat Stamper horse trade, one horse was enlarged with an air pump to appear healthier and heftier.

S. Wolff: Did he try to alter a horse's appearance to make it look better?

J. Faulkner: Yes, he would try to make a horse look good. He would put turpentine on the horse's hooves so it would step high. I've heard of it really happening, that about blowing up a horse, but I don't know whether Marvin was the one who did it.[17]

S. Wolff: Did you know a Suratt or a Ratliff?

J. Faulkner: Now, Mr. Hugh Miller Suratt really existed.

S. Wolff: Did he sell sewing machines?

J. Faulkner: No, he sold stoves out of the back of a truck. When Brother Will came out with a book using that name, Mr. Suratt called him and said: "If you don't change that name, the next voice you'll hear will be that of my attorney." That's when V. K. Ratliff came into being.[18]

F. Watkins: Let's look at some Faulkners. Back then the Falkners spelled their name without the *u*, correct?

J. Faulkner: Yes. Maud insisted on spelling her name without the *u*. In fact, she said, "Maud without the *e*, and Falkner without the *u*."

---

17. A similar occurrence takes place in *The Hamlet* during a deceptive horse-trading scheme.

18. See Pate, "Names of Characters," 222–23, for a discussion of the origin of the characters Ratliff and Suratt. In *The Faulkner-Cowley File: Letters and Memories, 1944–62,* ed. Malcolm Cowley (New York, 1966), 25–26, William Faulkner states he changed the name of his character Suratt to V. K. Ratliff because "a man of that name turned up at home, so I changed my man to Ratliff for the reason that my whole town spent much of its time trying to decide just what living man I was writing about." But see Cullen and Watkins, *Old Times,* 74, in which the authors claim that Faulkner based the characters Suratt and Ratliff on Lafayette County's most famous trader, June Suratt, who "turned up long before Faulkner created V. K. Suratt in his fiction . . . [and who traded] for anything he could make a sharp trade for—land, horses, sewing machines." But mainly he was a sewing-machine salesman.

See Blotner, *Faulkner: A Biography,* I, 545, for a discussion of the likeness of Hugh Miller Suratt to Faulkner's character V. K. Suratt, who became V. K. Ratliff. See also Elizabeth Kerr, *Yoknapatawpha: Faulkner's "Little Postage Stamp of Native Soil"* (New York, 1976), 129n118: "There is a connection between the two names which seems more than coincidental: according to the Military History of Mississippi W. T. Ratliff was a lieutenant in the First Regiment, Mississippi Artillery, and M. Surratt was Quartermaster in the Second Regiment, Infantry, of which William C. Falkner was Colonel." See also Marshall, "Scenes from Yoknapatawpha," 280–81. Ratliff appears in *The Hamlet* and other stories as a sewing-machine salesman. See Blotner, *Faulkner, A Biography,* II, 1010.

Figs. 20–22. John Falkner's tombstone, each side of which reflects his ambivalence about how he wished his name to be spelled. (*Photographs by Billy Howard*)

F. Watkins: Is there any special significance in the round top of this tombstone, or was that just the way the marble was carved at the time?

J. Faulkner: Well, a family picks up a habit, and that's what we did here.

This is Dean.[19] Brother Will wrote the epitaph, "I bear him on eagle's wings and brought him unto me." That's the same epitaph he put on John Sartoris' grave in *Sartoris* prior to Dean's death. He used the same one on his brother's grave, but he wrote it first for the fiction.

This is Brother Will's first daughter, 'Bama. She lived only five days. When she died, Brother Will brought her out here from his house to the cemetery with the coffin on his lap and buried her.[20] I don't think

19. Dean Swift Falkner, the youngest of William Faulkner's three brothers.

20. See Blotner, *Faulkner: A Biography,* I, 682, and Minter, *William Faulkner,* 127. See also Marshall, "Scenes from Yoknapatawpha," 165.

Aunt Estelle ever saw her in the coffin. John Cullen[21]—Jenks—made that enclosure around the grave, and Brother Will wouldn't let them put a name on it. He said, "She had not been in this world long enough to have acquired an identity."

F. Watkins: She was named Alabama?

J. Faulkner: Yes, Alabama.

F. Watkins: After the death of that child, that's also when he began drinking and went from here to Chapel Hill to New York to Jacksonville and back to New York. Estelle finally had to go get him.

J. Faulkner: I don't recall that. What I do recall is a misty January day, not cold, but damp, the day Alabama died. We knew things were bad. Uncle Ben Markette,[22] my cousin, brought a goat in to give milk to her. I remember being out in the back yard while they milked the goat. We had the goat there two or three days. Big Dad was still alive. He had a lot of influence on Brother Will's drinking. He kept him on an even keel following Alabama's death.

F. Watkins: Now, John and Sue,[23] who were they?

J. Faulkner: That's Uncle John, my granddaddy's brother. They lost two, three children. Aunt Sue, his wife, was my mother's first cousin; Uncle John was my daddy's uncle, making me double second cousins to these folks. When I was born, Aunt Sue walked in our room—they had just lost one of their children, I forget which—and looked at me and said, "He looks just like the last one I lost."

[Pointing.] This was Jack, the FBI man.

F. Watkins: Did he marry?

J. Faulkner: Yes, twice. He married Cecile Hargis, and they got along for eight or nine years, something like that, and she couldn't hack the FBI. So they called it quits, and that was when Jack was put on this

21. A native of Oxford, Mississippi, Cullen was a boyhood friend and later a hunting companion of William Faulkner's.

22. Jimmy's second cousin-in-law, Markette married Nina Murray, Lucille "Dolly" Ramey Falkner's maternal first cousin.

23. Sue Harkins, Jimmy's second cousin by relation to his mother, and his great-aunt by marriage to his great-uncle John.

special squad. Then World War II came along. He had been in the Marine Corps in World War I, and later through ROTC summer camps. He got a commission in the army. Having a law degree and being with the FBI, he was put in army intelligence and sent to North Africa. There he met Suzanne, a French actress. He married her and brought her back to the United States.[24] She's still alive and living in Mobile now. I go down about once every two months and see her—check on her.

F. Watkins: I see.

J. Faulkner: For a long time we couldn't speak English to her. She spoke only French, so Jack, who spoke French, interpreted for her.

F. Watkins: How old is she now?

J. Faulkner: She was a good bit younger than Jack. If I had to guess, I'd say sixty-two, three, four.

F. Watkins: Very young.

J. Faulkner: Real young. Now, let's walk on down this way. See that Stokes right over there, Miss Lilly Stokes. Here, back in the 1930s, during the drought that caused the Dust Bowl, Miss Lilly would go around to little towns in the area that were desperate for rain and make it rain by putting her feet in the water and sitting there till it rained.

One day she found out that she and Nanny were born on the same day. She came to see Nanny and said, "We could make a lot of money out of this if we go around together and put our feet in the water and make it rain." Nanny didn't believe that Miss Stokes could make it rain, so she said that she wouldn't go.

F. Watkins: I believe I've found a stranger name than "Snopes."

J. Faulkner: What?

F. Watkins: "Muckenfuss." There is also a man here named Wohlleben,[25] and they pronounced his name "Woolabun."

24. Falkner, *Falkners of Mississippi,* 177, 183–84.

25. An Oxford blacksmith whom Faulkner may have used as a source in *Requiem for a Nun,* in which a deserter from the Pennsylvania regiment, while riding a mule, captured a Federal payroll, made saddle blankets out of the uncut bills, and then hid them at home. The spelling of *Wohlleben* varies in cemetery and courthouse records. See Cullen and Watkins, *Old Times,* 74, for corroboration of this story.

J. Faulkner: Yes.

F. Watkins: He was supposed to have found a lot of sheets of uncut Federal currency and brought it back to Oxford under a horse blanket. Faulkner tells that story in *Requiem for a Nun.*

J. Faulkner: Yes. That's a true story. That was the raid on Grant's supply depot at Holly Springs that Van Dorn[26] made one night. Mr. Wohlleben was a blacksmith in Oxford. His blacksmith's shop was just down South Street about a block from the square on the east side, cater-cornered from where Smitty's cafe is. He, his wife, and four daughters lived in the back of the blacksmith shop. The girls were big-boned, husky women, except one. When the war came along, they put him in the cavalry, and he made that raid that night on Holly Springs to stop Grant's penetration into Vicksburg.

During the raid Wohlleben broke into the depot, which had just got these big sheets of uncut money in books like a Sears and Roebuck catalogue. They used to get them in sheets and cut them with scissors. The army paymasters had to cut the sheets to make the payroll for the troops.

Wohlleben got three of these books, these catalogs of uncut money; it could have been four bills across and five bills wide on one page. He put them under the saddle of his horse, under the saddle blanket, and then finished the raid. Later that night he rode back here to Oxford, about thirty miles south of Holly Springs, gave those books to his wife, and told her to bury them. He rode back to his unit, caught up with Van Dorn when he was going back up into Tennessee, and stayed with him. After the war he was the only man in Oxford who had any money.

F. Watkins: Who bought the Faulkner tombstones?

J. Faulkner: I did. Now, we are close to Mammy Callie's grave, and Brother Will's grave is right under those trees yonder. Want to walk?

26. On December 20, 1862, Maj. Gen. Earl Van Dorn led an attack on Gen. Ulysses S. Grant's supply station at Holly Springs, Mississippi. The attack was ordered by Lt. Gen. John C. Pemberton in an attempt to hinder Grant's efforts against Vicksburg. The attack, which lasted half a day, resulted in approximately $1.5 million in damage and the capture of about fifteen hundred Union soldiers (Patricia L. Faust, ed., *Historical Times Illustrated Encyclopedia of the Civil War* [New York, 1986] 365–66).

Fig. 23. Tombstone of Caroline Barr, "Mammy Callie," Faulkner's childhood caretaker and later friend (*Photograph by Billy Howard*)

F. Watkins: Yes.

J. Faulkner: Mammy Callie's is right yonder.

F. Watkins: Was this the black section of the graveyard?

J. Faulkner: Yes. [Passing a tall grave marker with stone carved into a sharp, vertical point.] The legend is that this grave stone has a point on it so that Yankees won't sit on it.

This is Mammy Callie. She and Brother Will's mother, Nanny, were the only people who could whip Brother Will when he was little. She helped raise him. She stayed with him. He was good to her, as she was to him. When she got old, he looked after her. The cabin in the back at Rowan Oak was built for Mammy Callie and Uncle Ned. Mammy Callie called Brother Will "Memi" [pronounced *me-me*]. As a child, Jack had tried to say "William," and his word came out "Memi," so that's what she called him.

She, my mother, and my grandmother were also the three who had the authority to whip me when I was a little boy. Now, Mammy Callie wasn't big—but, boy, could she whip!

S. Wolff: Did William Faulkner get whipped often?

J. Faulkner: Not that often.

S. Wolff: What might he have been whipped for?

J. Faulkner: Big Dad had a surrey, and he took Nanny for a Sunday afternoon ride. They left John, Jack, and Brother Will at home to play. The boys found a bucket of red paint. Brother Will got on top of a ladder, and John was on the bottom painting. They saw that they could flick paint, and the chickens, thinking the paint was food, would eat it. So they kept on flicking paint at the chickens.

When Nanny got home, she found the boys covered in paint. She immediately had the boys bathed in coal oil to get the paint off. But there wasn't much that could be done for the chickens. The paint got stiff, and the chickens began dragging their wings on the ground. Some of the chickens died. She said it wasn't worth leaving home anymore if she had to leave the boys by themselves. I imagine they all got a whipping for that.[27]

Brother Will subscribed to *Popular Mechanics*. He found out how to build a small steam engine, made one in the shed out back, and nearly burned the shed down. He had built a fire under it to make steam, so it would run. He was ten or twelve years old at the time.

Brother Will learned to make flash pictures at night. He had opened some shotgun shells to get the powder out and then lit the powder with a match. John was facing him with the pan in between them. Brother Will lit the powder for the flash, and John ended up with burned hair, eyebrows, and eyelashes.

Another time Brother Will built an airplane out in the back yard. He put his brother Jack in it and threw him off an embankment to see if it would fly. I don't think he got a whipping for any of these, because Big Dad and Nanny were feeling like they were defeated by all this.

S. Wolff: Will you tell the story of Mammy Callie's going and coming from Arkansas?

---

27. See Faulkner, *my brother Bill,* 39–40, and Blotner, *Faulkner: A Biography,* I, 112, for another example.

J. Faulkner: All right. Mammy Callie was always running off with some man to Arkansas.[28] Never the same one. She couldn't write, so she would send word back to Big Dad to come get her. She would catch some salesman on a train, and somehow the word would get back to Big Dad. Whatever he was doing, he would stop, go to Arkansas and get Mammy Callie, and bring her back.

One time he said, "Damn it, I'm just not going to do it anymore." She went off to Arkansas and sent word back again that she was ready to come home. Rather than going himself, he sent someone[29] to get her. This man went over and found Mammy Callie sitting in the depot waiting. They got on the train and came home.

S. Wolff: What did she say when she arrived at home?

J. Faulkner: She told Big Dad, "If you don't think enough of me to come get me yourself, I'm not going to leave anymore." [Laughter.] And she didn't!

F. Watkins: How old was she when she died in 1940?

J. Faulkner: One hundred years. Brother Will held her funeral in his living room at Rowan Oak and then brought her out here and buried her.

F. Watkins: He did not preach orthodox Christian theology, did he?

J. Faulkner: It was more personal.

F. Watkins: Was it irreverent?

J. Faulkner: Oh, no, no, no. Of course not.

F. Watkins: But it didn't follow a rigid creed.

J. Faulkner: Not really. He wasn't much for orthodoxy.

F. Watkins: Do you think he believed in God? I don't know if I've ever asked you this question, and there have been so many answers, I don't know what you'd say. What do you think William Faulkner thought of God?

J. Faulkner: Have you ever read *The Revelations of Louise?*[30]

F. Watkins: No.

28. See Faulkner, *my brother Bill,* 48–49.
29. John Falkner's account names this individual as Mr. Bennett (*ibid.,* 49).
30. Albert Stevens Crockett, *The Revelations of Louise* (New York, 1920).

J. Faulkner: All right. Let me tell you this, and then I'll tell you what he thought. Some girl, eighteen, nineteen years old, died about 1917 or early 1918. She felt herself go away from her body, and people were crying because of her death. She was trying to get back to them to tell them that she was happy with friends and not to be sad.

The book is based on this, and Louise said that when people died, there are friends and family waiting to help them through. At one point in the book, they ask Louise, through a medium, "Is there anyone else here?" She said, "The room is full." They said to Louise, "How many people are in this room with you?" She said, "Over five thousand."

Now, I'll get back to Brother Will. He had a photographic mind. Anything he ever read, he never forgot. He didn't put on a show of being religious. He didn't read the Bible all the time—a lot of people read the Bible once a day, once a month, once a year, something like that. When he was young, he read it, and he could quote any part of it. So why read it again?

Well, John, Chooky, Jack, Brother Will, and I were sitting on the steps of the old Oxford hospital. This was in October, 1960, and Nanny was dying; we knew that she only had a few days to live. Jack said, "Bill, how do you think you'll recognize Dad when you're going to be older than he is?" Brother Will said, "Jack, the way I feel about it is that we all will probably be little radio waves. Something like little radio waves."[31] Well, that's the soul, just as it is described in *The Revelations of Louise.* That's why you can get five thousand little radio waves in one little room. Is that sort of an answer?

F. Watkins: Yes.

J. Faulkner: It's the best I can do. Y'all want a sermon?

F. Watkins: It's better than I can do.

S. Wolff: Would you say that William Faulkner was ever a religious man in a more traditional sense?

J. Faulkner: He was a religious man; he really was, very much so. But he didn't make a big show of it. He only went to church twice a year—Christmas and Easter. But he was a Christian—a real believer.

31. "Maybe each of us will become some sort of radio wave" (Falkner, *Falkners of Mississippi,* 189).

F. Watkins: I remember reading that Jack did quote the passage on the radio waves in his book—was it called *The Falkner Family?*

J. Faulkner: The Falkners of Mississippi. Yes, there are a few of us around.

S. Wolff: Has your entire family been buried in this graveyard?

J. Faulkner: Since we came here in 1885, yes. Now, see this mausoleum over here?

F. Watkins: Yes.

J. Faulkner: Lokey Lynch lived here in Oxford. His daddy walked back from Gettysburg with a minie ball in his knee. They told him that they were going to have to take his leg off. He said, "You're not going to take my leg off. I'm going to die with that leg on." The doc said, "Well, it's not going to be long." I remember the old man. He was ninety-six when he died; he still had that minie ball in his knee. Anyway, Lokey built that mausoleum when his wife died in the late 1930s. It was the worst-looking thing; it still is. The grave plot is marked right there.

F. Watkins: Most graves are buried east and west.

J. Faulkner: There's one that's not. They say he was a convict, and he didn't deserve to be buried east-west.

F. Watkins: That was true of a man in my home town; a convict was buried north-south, and then his grave was lost. The disgrace in being buried north and south is that, since the sun rises in the east and sets in the west, on Resurrection Day, the sun will come up in the east; you'll rise up, face the Lord, and, if you're north and south, you're going to be looking the wrong way. [Laughter.]

J. Faulkner: Have you heard the story about the drunk who staggered through the graveyard and fell off in a grave?

F. Watkins: No.

J. Faulkner: He finally sobered up the next morning, and he looked around and saw that he was in a graveyard. He said, "Well, it's Judgment Day, and I am the first one up." [Laughter.]

F. Watkins: Have you seen those little wooden houses in country graveyards? My great-uncle got drunk one Saturday night and crawled in after it started raining. He went to sleep in it. He slept in it all night and woke up the next morning. Church services were going, and the choir was singing. He was scared to death because he knew it was Resurrection morning, and he'd died drunk. That's true.

J. Faulkner: Now, I'll tell you, that's a tough part of the country, down in Dallas, south of Yocona; and if they didn't kill a fellow on Saturday night, they didn't have a good weekend at all. There was a man down there—he was a renegade, drunk, and everything—and he died. They took his casket and headed to church. The folks at the door said, "We couldn't help him before he died; we can't help him now." They wouldn't let him in.

F. Watkins: They wouldn't let him in!

Malcolm Franklin is buried here, isn't he?

J. Faulkner: Yes.

F. Watkins: Were some of his papers recently given to the University of South Carolina?

[Approaching the grave of William Faulkner.]

J. Faulkner: Yes. Now, here is the grave of William Faulkner.

S. Wolff: Did he choose this epitaph?

J. Faulkner: I'm not sure he said what he wanted on his tombstone. I think he said, "He made the books, and he died. That's the way I want to be remembered." He also said, "I wish thirty years ago I could have looked forward and not signed anything."

F. Watkins: Who chose the epitaph "Beloved, go with God"?

J. Faulkner: Aunt Estelle. I was sitting there when she did it, and it sure was a funny feeling when she said that.

F. Watkins: Did Estelle do that against his wishes?

J. Faulkner: He just said he would be remembered as the man who wrote the books, and that's all.

F. Watkins: You see, half of that remark, "he made the books," was so deadly serious—but that's not the whole William Faulkner. The other half was having fun at the same time.

Fig. 24. William Faulkner's tombstone (*Photograph by Billy Howard*)

Fig. 25. The inscription on William Faulkner's tombstone (*Photograph by Billy Howard*)

J. Faulkner: He made a statement one time—I forget the way he put it—"Country folks are my lot; I'd rather be with them."[32]

F. Watkins: Did William resent the people in his hometown not knowing much about him?

J. Faulkner: No, he was real proud of it; he'd rather they didn't.

Yes, he was private, all right. He often wore an old pair of pants that he had just torn to make shorts out of and an old sweatshirt that he had torn the sleeves out of. He really looked like a sharecropper, or worse. He had an old pair of farm shoes, and he wore brown socks with the white toes and white cuffs on the socks.

One time some people came up to Brother Will at his house and asked him questions about Mr. Faulkner, and he said, "I don't know anything about him. I just work here." They just turned around and left. When he didn't want to be bothered, he ignored people. His moods would surprise you.[33]

I was real careful not to let anybody get to him through me. One time I was going across the square by Uncle John's law office. Uncle John yelled at me to come up to his office. When I got up there, he said, "Jim, there's a boy here doing his dissertation on my granddaddy," meaning the Old Colonel. "Take him down to see Bill. He'll talk to him." I said, "All right," and headed down to Brother Will's. When we got in the driveway, I said, "Brother Will might talk to you, or he might not. I don't know. If he doesn't, there's not a damn thing I can do about it."

So, even though I didn't like to do this—because I knew Brother Will didn't like it—I left the man in the car, and I went in and said, "Brother Will, Uncle John told me to bring this man I left in the car to talk to you; it wasn't any of my doing." Brother Will said, "Well, bring

---

32. "I have met one or two people—a photographer, and real painter. He is going to have an exhibition in New York in the fall, and he sure can paint. I dont like the place I am living in. Its full of dull middle class very polite conventional people. Too much like being at a continual reception. Country folks are my sort, anyway. So I am going to move next week. I think I can live cheaper than $1.50 per day" (William C. Faulkner to Mrs. M. C. Falkner, August 16, 1925, Letter 15 in *Selected Letters of William Faulkner*, ed. Joseph Blotner [New York, 1978], 12).

33. See Faulkner, *my brother Bill*, 226, on William Faulkner's unapproachableness.

him in." They talked for an hour. The dissertation is called "Son of Sorrow," by Don Duclos.[34] But it was a very rare occurrence that Brother Will would talk to anybody he didn't know well.

F. Watkins: Did William Faulkner like Mac Reed?[35] Was Mac Reed the close friend Faulkner made him out to be?

J. Faulkner: Yes, Mr. Mac Reed, of Gathright-Reed Drugstore, has got to be the epitome of a southern gentleman. He was a real close friend. Real close. I don't believe the man ever had a bad thought in his mind. He was a sergeant in World War I. On Armistice Day in 1918, he shot an anvil.

S. Wolff: What does that mean—to "shoot an anvil"?

J. Faulkner: What you do is tie two blacksmith's anvils together, one anvil upside down with the other anvil on top of it. Each anvil has a hole in its bottom. Fill the holes full of powder. Then tie the anvils together and shoot. The sound from the powder exploding will rattle windows for a long way around. It makes a loud noise like a cannon. Loud noise. Loud enough to make stock break out of the lot. He shot the anvil just to celebrate Armistice Day.

34. Donald Philip Duclos, "Son of Sorrow: The Life, Works and Influence of Colonel William C. Falkner, 1825–1889" (Ph.D. dissertation, University of Michigan, 1962).

35. William "Mac" McNeil Reed, Faulkner's friend at the Gathright-Reed Drugstore, where Faulkner traded. See Faulkner, *my brother Bill,* 237, for further details. William McNeil Reed's daughter confirmed the spelling of her father's nickname as *Mac* (Carolyn R. McGuire to Sally Wolff, August 10, 1993).

3

OUT IN THE COUNTY:
YOKNAPATAWPHA REVISITED

They hadn't never seen the river so high, and it's not done raining yet.
There was old men that hadn't never seen nor heard of it being so in the
memory of man.

—*As I Lay Dying*

All that remained of him was the river bed which his slaves had straightened for almost ten miles to keep his land from flooding.

—*The Hamlet*

*Images of the country pervade Faulkner's Yoknapatawpha novels:
weathered boards on one-lane bridges, shotgun and dogtrot houses, the
rough-hewn, wooden elegance of plantation residences, the country
stores, the dark woods and dirt roads of Frenchman's Bend, rivers that
crawl slowly in summer and, in times of turbulent weather, relentlessly
sweep their banks clear.*

*Exploring some of the rural sources of Faulkner's fiction, Jimmy
Faulkner discusses the name of the Yocona River, its history, and the similarity of the fictional and real counties in which hills, river bends, dogtrot
houses, and country stores call to mind Faulkner scenes or stories.*

YOCONA RIVER

J. Faulkner: We're in the area Brother Will knew well. In *As I Lay Dying*, when they were trying to get Addie Bundren buried, the Bundren family traveled in the southeast part of the county on the south side of the Yocona River. We've been on the south side of the Yocona River Bridge, south of the little village of Markette. The Bundrens finally crossed the river, right down here where we're going to cross the Yocona River at the Taylor Bridge, so Anse Bundren could get a new wife and a new set of teeth. We're going to cross the railroad track down through Taylor in the western part of the county. This would be an area like the Bundrens lived in.

F. Watkins: Is this the Yoknapatawpha?[1]

J. Faulkner: Yes.

F. Watkins: Where are we in relation to Taylor?

J. Faulkner: We are standing on a bridge over the Old Yocona River Run about two miles south of Taylor. Taylor is about six miles south of Oxford. The new channel that carries the Yocona River now is about a half a mile south of where we are. We are about seven miles south of Oxford on the road to Water Valley, where a road forks off to the southwest to Taylor about three or four miles away from here. My mother's cousin, John Markette, posted a sign on his land near here that says, No Trespassing! Survivors Will Be Prosecuted.

F. Watkins: That's right generous of him to put that up there.

J. Faulkner: Yes. There ain't many of the Markettes left.

F. Watkins: This is still more or less Yocona Bottom, isn't it?[2]

J. Faulkner: That's the Yocona River, right there. It runs through the Markette place. The Markettes have about three thousand acres here.

---

1. Blotner suggests that the original river was called the Yocanapatafa. See Blotner, *Faulkner: A Biography*, I, 73, and Cullen and Watkins, *Old Times*, 84. See also two letters appearing in the *East Tennessee Historical Society*, XXX (1958), 98, and XXXI (1959), 69, which refer to the historical name of the river as the Yockeny Petafa and the Yockny Pattafan.

2. The term *bottom* refers to the fertile, flat land near the basin of the river.

Fig. 26. The Yocona River, *ca.* 1970s (*Courtesy of the Floyd C. Watkins Collection, Special Collections Department, Robert W. Woodruff Library, Emory University*)

F. Watkins: The Yocona? That's short for Yoknapatawpha, right? Historically, I guess this river has been spelled ten, twenty different ways.

J. Faulkner: Yes, I'm sure it has.

F. Watkins: In my book I have a copy of the drainage district tax receipt spelling Yoknapatawpha exactly like that of the county.[3]

J. Faulkner: This area is known still as the Yocona Drainage District.

F. Watkins: There was a tax on that, right?

J. Faulkner: Yes.

F. Watkins: What were the taxes used for?

J. Faulkner: To cut the channel and to drain the Yocona River bottom to cut down on the flooding.

F. Watkins: Who paid the tax?

J. Faulkner: Landowners who had farms and benefited from the drainage district. The tax was prorated by the acre.

3. See Floyd C. Watkins, *In Time and Place* (Athens, Ga., 1977), 174.

Fig. 27. Floyd Watkins' 1949 Pontiac on an old bridge over the Yocona River in 1957. This crossing may be the source for the place where the Bundrens crossed. A modern, concrete structure replaced this bridge in the early 1980s. (*Courtesy of the Floyd C. Watkins Collection, Special Collections Department, Robert W. Woodruff Library, Emory University*)

F. Watkins: Did you ever find any arrowheads down here?

J. Faulkner: I never have, but other people have.

F. Watkins: I was just looking up on the bluff. I'll bet that's a good place to find them.

J. Faulkner: They get them up on the bluffs, not there in the bottom, after a rain has washed some dirt away and uncovered them.

[Driving down the length of the river, Jimmy points out one of the few places at which a crossing would have been possible. At such a place, he speculates, the Bundrens might have crossed the fictional counterpart to this river in *As I Lay Dying*.]

F. Watkins: Now, is this still the Old Yocona River Run?

J. Faulkner: Yes.

F. Watkins: So the bridge, where the Bundrens might have gone, had to cross this river?[4]

J. Faulkner: This crossing or the one down yonder. In the novel the Bundrens came from an area like this. They were also working in an area like this when they were trying to get across the flooded Yocona River.

F. Watkins: But do you think that the Bundrens would have crossed it before it was straightened or after it was straightened?

J. Faulkner: I would say before.

F. Watkins: What is the source for the Bundren family? Is the area they lived in around here?

J. Faulkner: The Bundren family was partially based on a family who lived south of the Yocona River in the southeast part of the county. Junior Tidwell, a person who lived around here, may also have been the basis for one of the Bundren children. Junior's a different sort of guy. He set the woods on fire, and, finally, he burned himself up.

S. Wolff: What did he look like?

J. Faulkner: He always carried a tow sack over his shoulder, and it seemed like he'd never shave—well, he'd shave, but I never saw him when he didn't have about a four- or five-day growth of beard on his face, and he was never clean. He wore a train fireman's hat, overalls with them rolled up about calf high, and he'd wear big, old brogans and carry anything that he'd pick up in that tow sack.

One time Junior stopped at the store and said that he wanted to buy a hoe to use for chopping cotton.[5] Mrs. Brown gave him a hoe and said, as Junior was leaving, "Junior, you haven't paid me for that hoe." He said, "I ain't chopped no cotton yet, neither." [Laughter.]

S. Wolff: Where did the Tidwells live?

J. Faulkner: South of the Yocona River and east of Highway 7 in the southeast part of the county.

---

4. See *As I Lay Dying*, in which the Bundren family must forge this tumultuous river to carry Addie's coffin to Jefferson to be buried.

5. Chop cotton: to chop weeds between the rows of cotton.

S. Wolff: Do you know anyone with the name Bundren?

J. Faulkner: Yes. I know some folks named Bundren. Some of these Bundrens moved to town, and one ran a filling station and small country store with a gas pump in front. The store was about three miles west of Taylor and had a sign on the front saying "Bundren Store."

S. Wolff: Is Bundren a common name in the county?

J. Faulkner: Yes, in the south part of the county.

[A new concrete river bridge replaces the one-lane, wooden bridge on the Old Yocona River in the west-central part of Lafayette County.]

J. Faulkner: We are a couple of miles south of the town of Taylor. Brother Will described this river as it was before the channel was cut. The channel was cut to make the water run faster and drain off sooner. It left cutoffs in the old river run where water still stands. I used to fish in it. Let's go on the other side.

This is the Old Yocona River Run before they channeled it. A wooden bridge used to cross the old river run, but, now, there is a concrete bridge over the channel. Because of the channeling, the water does not move anymore, except when it rains and the water runs off.

F. Watkins: The water, even in the dry season, would have been coming much faster than this slow flow.

J. Faulkner: The channel being straight allows the water to run faster than in a curving river and allows the high water to drain quicker. The bends in the river make the water run slower, so the water backs up and rises sooner and higher. That caused the wooden bridges over the river on the lower crossings to float off their foundations and sometimes move with the current downstream.[6]

F. Watkins: It's very straight for long distances, now.

J. Faulkner: Yes. The Yocona River is not very long. It starts right around Tula, about ten or twelve miles east of here. Then, of course, the Enid Reservoir is about five miles down west of here. From there the

6. In *As I Lay Dying*, the Bundrens cross a turbulent and fast-moving river. Today, following the channeling, the river meanders quietly.

water flows into the Yalobusha River to form the Yazoo River close to Greenwood.

There's a copperhead! That's a copperhead! Now, look at that snake!

F. Watkins: That one was probably a spreading adder.

J. Faulkner: We call them a hog nose. They spread their heads, flatten it, and make it very wide. It looks like a cobra.

F. Watkins: Isn't that the only snake indigenous to North America that spreads?

J. Faulkner: Yes, I think so. Now, look over here. You can see the volume of water that comes through the Yocona River in the channel.

F. Watkins: They did this straightening before they had mechanical engines, right?

J. Faulkner: Yes, I guess so. That's a coon track right there, just on the other side of that rock.

F. Watkins: They had to work with mules and slips—animal equipment—and they straightened this river out for how many miles, Jimmy?

J. Faulkner: Probably fifteen.

F. Watkins: Fifteen miles! In *The Hamlet,* Faulkner says that the old Frenchman Grenier[7] had his slaves straighten the river.

J. Faulkner: Do you know why this is called Frenchman's Bend?[8] In the French and Indian War, a troop of French soldiers camped in the bend of the Yocona River. They thought they were safe, but the Indians slipped in that night and killed them all. The old-timers referred to it at first as the bend where the Frenchmen were killed and then just Frenchman's Bend.

F. Watkins: Doesn't this river have a terrible reputation for flooding?

J. Faulkner: Yes, it does. This is where I've seen the river hill to hill, even before they had a dam.

7. "The Huguenot younger son who brought the first slaves into the country and was granted the first big land patent and so became the first cotton planter" (William Faulkner, *Requiem for a Nun,* 7).
8. A community on the Yoknapatawpha River in Faulkner's county.

F. Watkins: What do you mean "hill to hill"?

J. Faulkner: Well, I can show you: The river runs between these two large hill lines. I've seen the river rise up to the foot of this hill all the way to the foot of the hill on the other side of the river, and people couldn't get across.

F. Watkins: What would cause the great flooding in this valley?

J. Faulkner: The runoff, the amount of drainage area it had, and heavy spring rains. Willow trees along the bank would hold water, and the river would keep backing up and backing up.

F. Watkins: The flooding in this river was greater than in the bottom of the Tallahatchie?

J. Faulkner: Yes.

F. Watkins: Or any other river that you know of flowing east of the Mississippi?

J. Faulkner: Yes, actually.

F. Watkins: Would that be the background for the flood in *As I Lay Dying*?

J. Faulkner: Could be, could very well be. Any meandering in a river like that slows water down, and it can't run off fast. That's why they cut a channel.

F. Watkins: Where would you find more fish—in this old run here or in the channel out there?

J. Faulkner: Probably in the channel because it drains more from the creeks and streams around Tula that run into it from both sides. The Yocona River gets some of its water from the middle of University Avenue in Oxford. University Avenue is on the dividing line between the Tallahatchie watershed and the Yocona watershed. Water flowing south goes to the Yocona River. The water on the other side, going north, goes to the Tallahatchie River.

F. Watkins: I see.

J. Faulkner: The Tallahatchie is a bigger, deeper river, and longer.

F. Watkins: Faulkner, of course, himself went to the Tallahatchie much more than he ever came to the Yocona.

J. Faulkner: Yes, because he hunted up there more than back down here.

F. Watkins: You mean at Frenchman's Bend?

J. Faulkner: In the Yocona River bottom.

[Continuing to drive up the length of the river and approaching the former town of Yocona.]

F. Watkins: That's not part of the Yocona there, too, is it?

J. Faulkner: That's Pumpkin Creek; we are close to the town of Yocona, about six or seven miles southeast of Oxford on the Old Pontotoc Road. Yocona was a nice little old town, too, until they took the school and post office away from it.

F. Watkins: There was a town Yocona?

J. Faulkner: Yes.

F. Watkins: Where was it?

J. Faulkner: The Yocona River starts in the eastern part of the county, close to Tula, which could have been the area like the one from which Flem Snopes might have come. It flows almost due west, passing one or two miles south of Yocona, the town, and it flows on, passing south of Taylor, and leaves Lafayette County. It was dammed up at Enid to make the reservoir. We'll go through the town of Yocona up here.

F. Watkins: It wasn't just losing the school or the post office that caused the end of the town. It was the fact that you could go to Oxford or Memphis in your truck on Saturday.

J. Faulkner: All of those things, but with gasoline going up, it could bring these little country towns back. Now, we are coming to the little town of Yocona, right here.

Now, we're approaching Lafayette Springs in the eastern part of Lafayette County, and this used to be a summer resort. At one time there was a big, wooden hotel located here, and the people would come from all around. The spring was supposed to help your health. I think the hotel sat right out here someplace; people would spend their summers here.

F. Watkins: Is this the section Faulkner called the Pine Woods?

J. Faulkner: Yes, that is where we are right now. East and northeastern Lafayette County.

S. Wolff: Earlier you showed us William Faulkner's fishing license. Did he fish much?

J. Faulkner: Yes, he did. He didn't fish much in his later life. He was a fly fisherman. He sent us out one time to catch a lot of fish for a barbecue, and he knew dang well that we couldn't catch enough fish in one night for all that. We caught only one. We spent all night on the creek just for that one fish.

S. Wolff: Did you fish with him?

J. Faulkner: I'd go with him. I was too little to do much fishing at that time, but I really liked to swim better. I used to take my .22 rifle and hack away at snakes, turtles, and things like that. I fished with him, yes.

S. Wolff: What kind of fish did he like to catch?

J. Faulkner: Bass and trout, mostly. He would fish in Hedleston Lake by College Hill and Temple's Lake. That's not too far from Oxford—southeast of Oxford a little ways.

S. Wolff: Did you fish for catfish?

J. Faulkner: Yes.

S. Wolff: You both did?

J. Faulkner: I did. He did, too. He'd fish for anything, but mostly he did fly fishing or casting. I'd get a long cane pole with a hook and worms, and I'd fish for catfish.

S. Wolff: Was he a good fisherman?

J. Faulkner: Yes, pretty good.

S. Wolff: Are you?

J. Faulkner: Not really. [Laughter.] I spend my time hunting. Fishing doesn't really send me too far.

THE NATCHEZ TRACE, YELLOWLEAF CREEK, AND RIVERS HILL

That afternoon we built the stock pen. We built it deep in the creek bottom, where you could not have found it unless you had known where to look, and you could not have seen it until you came to the new sap-sweating, axe-ended rails woven through and into the jungle growth itself.

—*The Unvanquished*

Touring more of Lafayette County, particularly locations that may have inspired certain scenes in William Faulkner's novels, Jimmy points out sites such as Grandma Harkins' farm. A tale similar to the Civil War story of hiding her cattle in the creek bottom appears in The Unvanquished. *Jimmy also discusses the Natchez Trace, once a freighters' and travelers' trail that extends from Natchez to Nashville; Yellowleaf Creek, which Faulkner renamed Whiteleaf Creek in his fiction; and Rivers Hill, a site near Oxford similar to that where Pat Stamper's horse trade took place in* The Hamlet. *The variety of snakes Jimmy identifies and the cacophony of sounds in the air—quail calling, dogs barking, chickens squawking—are constant reminders of the surrounding country landscape.*

[Near Yellowleaf Creek.]

F. Watkins: Now, would this be cotton land, soybean, or what?

J. Faulkner: Either one. That's a pretty field there.

F. Watkins: Does it always have variegated colors?

J. Faulkner: Only after rain.

S. Wolff: Would you explain the contour farming in this area?

J. Faulkner: Contour farming is where you plow your rows around a hill or valley and keep the same elevation all the time so that when it rains the water will not run off fast and wash land away.

A man named Jake Smith farms here in the northeast part of Lafayette County. He does the reverse of sharecropping—the way farming used to be done here a long time ago. Sharecroppers worked small plots of land and paid a share to the landowner. But this man rents or works on shares, and he has all the equipment. He farms about five thousand acres of land and pays in shares the same as old times. But he does all the work on a lot of farms. He's the big farmer now, where the landowner used to be. Their positions are reversed.

S. Wolff: Is that common in the area?

J. Faulkner: Yes. You can't buy this big equipment and pay a lot of money for it unless you have plenty of land to farm. So he might farm ten, twelve farms with his equipment.

Fig. 28. Yellowleaf Creek, which Faulkner renames Whiteleaf
Creek in his novels (*Photograph by Billy Howard*)

Now, we have just crossed Yellowleaf Creek. It is east of Oxford
toward Pontotoc. Yellowleaf Creek starts east of Oxford and flows
south into the Yocona River approximately seven miles south of Oxford
and crosses the Old Pontotoc Road about two or three miles southeast of
Oxford. Brother Will renamed it Whiteleaf Creek where it crosses Old
Highway 6 up yonder.[9]

    F. Watkins: Yes. Now, this area is like that in *The Unvanquished*
where Granny hid her horses?[10]

    J. Faulkner: Yes, we are on the Fudgetown Road that runs east
and west a mile or two north of the Yocona River between the Water
Valley Road and Old Pontotoc Road.

    We are now on what used to be the farm of my great-grandmother,
Grandma Harkins, my mother's grandmother. She had a farm on this
north side of the Yocona River. Her husband was in a POW camp during the Civil War. He had been captured early in the war, and she was

    9. See Faulkner's *Hamlet*, 34 and elsewhere.
   10. Faulkner, *The Unvanquished*, 12.

Fig. 29. Land along this treeline belonged to Grandma Harkins, Jimmy Faulkner's great-grandmother. Among these trees she hid her livestock from the Yankees. Faulkner chronicles a similar story in *The Unvanquished*. (*Photograph by Billy Howard*)

keeping the farm together. One time, when the Yankees came through, she asked one of them to take a blanket to her husband. The northern soldier said, "I would, but he would never get it." Grandma Harkins had no hard feelings and said he was the only good Yankee.

She also did her best to keep her stock fat and in good shape. The people at the next farm had stock sort of like the Snopeses' stock; they would feed them when they wanted to, and they wouldn't feed them when they didn't want to. So they were weak and run down. When the Federal troops came through, Grandma Harkins took her stock—mules, cows, and horses—down to the Yocona Bottom and hid them in the long sweep of land down along the river.

When the troops went to take the neighbor's stock, they said, "If you won't take ours, we'll tell you where better stock is." So they told the Yankees, who then took all of Grandma Harkins' stock and didn't bother the neighbor's. That family and ours haven't gotten along since 1863.

F. Watkins: Did William Faulkner know that at the time when he wrote *The Unvanquished* about Granny's hiding her stock?

J. Faulkner: Oh, yes, yes.

F. Watkins: Do you think he had it in mind, or do you think it was a coincidence of everybody hiding stock?

J. Faulkner: A little of both.

[Driving past Grandma Harkins' farm.]

See those horses? I haven't seen a mule down here in a long time. I'm sure there are some. They about died out when the tractors came up; nobody needed them anymore. People over in New Albany raise mules, but it has gotten to be a sport. A contest sport. The price of a mule is way up there now. Once you could buy a pretty good mule for fifty dollars. Now, they go as high as fifteen to twenty thousand dollars. Really strong mules—they haul them around and dress them up. The ones that are strong enough to pull the weight will win the contest.

F. Watkins: This is Water Valley. What is the county seat of Yalobusha County?

J. Faulkner: They have two county seats down there, Coffeeville and Water Valley. The reason is that the Skuna River runs between them, and in the wintertime it flooded. The people on the south side of the county couldn't get to Water Valley, and the people on the north side of the county couldn't get to Coffeeville. They put one courthouse in one part of the county and another on the other side; so they had two county seats—and still have.

We are now fifty miles from the Natchez Trace. Outlaws used to hold up merchants who traveled the trace. The people who used the Natchez Trace moved between Natchez and Nashville. There was also a group of brothers who operated between Jackson and Natchez, but I'm not sure.[11]

11. See Faulkner's account of these Natchez Trace outlaw empires of Hare and Mason, the mad Harpe brothers, and Murrell in Faulkner, *Requiem for a Nun.*

S. Wolff: Eudora Welty's *The Robber Bridegroom* is about those same brothers.

[A large snake lies in the road.]

F. Watkins: Look, there's a snake. He's still alive; look at him.

J. Faulkner: No, he's dead, but not dead too long.

F. Watkins: Is that a water snake?

J. Faulkner: No, that's a chicken snake. They have a dozen kinds of names, such as grass snake. Remember our referring to Pat Stamper in *The Hamlet* who traded horses?

S. Wolff: Yes.

J. Faulkner: This is Rivers Hill, the location like the one where Pat Stamper was when they came to Jefferson to get the cream separator in *The Hamlet*. This location was named for Mag Rivers; she was a black woman who took in the wash. She would pick up a basketful of laundry and balance it on her head. Never put her hands on it. She would walk all the way from our house on University Avenue that way. You can see Oxford from the top of the hill.

S. Wolff: Doesn't one of your father's paintings depict a wash woman with laundry balanced on her head?

J. Faulkner: Yes, that's right.

F. Watkins: Was there a source for the wen that fell off the Young Colonel?[12]

J. Faulkner: This is what happened. There was a wen—you know, a bump on his face—and it was Will Falls, the character, who put this stuff on his face.

S. Wolff: Will Falls got the recipe for the medicine from an old Choctaw woman.

J. Faulkner: A conglomerate of axle grease and stuff like that made a salve. The salve had been on his face for a while. Auntee, the Young Colonel's daughter, forced him, or just badgered him, until he

12. See Blotner, *Faulkner: A Biography,* I, 144, 544–45. This event occurs fictitiously in *Flags in the Dust.* According to Jimmy Faulkner, Dr. Ashford Little treated the Young Colonel's wen.

went to the doctor. It was a young doctor, who had just come to town, who said the wen was going to kill him if he didn't get to a specialist. So he reached up to touch it, and it fell off in his hand and left shiny new skin. So the concoction worked. Later on the doctor and Brother Will got to be pretty good friends.

Now, this was the town of Markette about seven miles south of Oxford. There was an old store and post office back here at one time.

F. Watkins: Is this the Yocona Bottom?

J. Faulkner: Yes, this is Yocona Bottom.

F. Watkins: There's a hawk flying, but you can't kill him.

J. Faulkner: Do you know—I expect that's true. You can be fined for picking bluebells in Texas, too!

F. Watkins: On your own place?

J. Faulkner: Anywhere, yes! You can't kill a hawk; you can't protect your chickens; you can't do anything except shoot birds or animals in season. It's gotten to the point where the state is controlling too damn much.

F. Watkins: I can imagine what your Uncle Will would think about that.

J. Faulkner: Right.

F. Watkins: How big is Lafayette County?

J. Faulkner: It's about forty miles square. The way they laid the county out was—they figured about how long it would take a man to ride from home leaving at daylight on a horse to the county seat, do a couple of hours of business, and ride home on the same horse by dark.

DOGTROT HOUSE

It was dusk. He emerged from the bottom and looked up the slope of his meagre and sorry corn and saw it—the paintless two room cabin with an open hallway between and a lean-to kitchen . . . which was just like the one he had been born in which had not belonged to his father either, and just like the one he would die in if he died indoors.

—*The Hamlet*

Seeing a dogtrot house initiates a discussion of country people and their quality of life and of people who lived in this style of house. One of the most common structures in rural Lafayette County in the nineteenth century, the dogtrot is now a rarity in the countryside. This particular house is one of the only remaining structures of its type in the county. The decline of the dogtrot exemplifies the passing of the rural way of life that Faulkner depicts.

[A few miles east of Oxford near Yellowleaf Creek.]

J. Faulkner: There's a dogtrot house.[13] That one's got tar paper around it. See it?

F. Watkins: Yes. Now, this is pretty poor country here. Was it always unpopulated?

J. Faulkner: No, a lot of this part of the country just west of Oxford had big farms and little farms, and, right in here, these hills out here were settled by people from the hills of east Tennessee. They were used to little farms, and back then it just didn't take a heck of a lot for them to get along. The bigger farms were out in the western part of the county.

F. Watkins: So big farms were out on the Yocona in the western part of the country? What about up on the Tallahatchie?

J. Faulkner: Even up on the Tallahatchie, they had some, but the Tallahatchie was not cleared out as early as the southern part of the county because you are getting to more delta down that way. The Tallahatchie has got real good bottom.

The Tallahatchie up north of here was a treacherous river. The big eddy is down there near General Stone's hunting camp cabin, and everybody is scared of that thing. If you get caught in it, you'll go under.

F. Watkins: Take your boat under?

J. Faulkner: Yes.

13. This type of house, usually built with logs, popular in the nineteenth-century South, has a breezeway separating the two sections of the house, each consisting of a single room. The dogtrot house could be altered by enclosing the open passage.

Fig. 30. A typical dogtrot house (*Courtesy of the Floyd C. Watkins Collection, Special Collections Department, Robert W. Woodruff Library, Emory University*)

F. Watkins: I wonder how deep it is.

S. Wolff: [Looking at the house.] The open passageway of a dogtrot part of a house like this one would be for ventilation primarily and separation of the parents from the older children.

J. Faulkner: And separation of the sleeping from eating.

S. Wolff: Do high ceilings in the larger houses in town serve a similar purpose in ventilating?

J. Faulkner: Yes, the old, big houses had twelve-foot ceilings that were built for coolness in the summertime. We could handle winter. We could chop wood all the time. We didn't have air conditioning, and we didn't have a place to plug our fan into. Sometimes we'd sit outside at night waiting for the place to cool off, then go inside and go to bed.

S. Wolff: Could you describe the construction of the dogtrot houses and the resources the people had who lived in them?

J. Faulkner: The rooms in a dogtrot were divided up into housing areas—sleeping, eating, living. The tenants didn't have much money to

Fig. 31. The open passageway between the two rooms of the dogtrot house (*Photograph by Billy Howard*)

Fig. 32. An old outhouse in northern Mississippi (*Courtesy of the Floyd C. Watkins Collection, Special Collections Department, Robert W. Woodruff Library, Emory University*)

build with. There was no place to buy anything. So they built with what they had or could make. They even made nails and shingles on the place—wooden shingles and everything for these old houses.

If somebody came here with a hundred dollars, he would be rich. He could put in a crop and build a house. People began to get a lot of money when they shipped cotton down the river. The site of one of the biggest shipping ports is across the way at Wyatt's Crossing. That was a shipping trail for cotton before the war.

S. Wolff: So the people here were mostly cotton farmers?

J. Faulkner: Yes. In the east part of the county—the hill part of the county—were small farms. Maybe ten, twelve, or fifteen acres were cotton, and they lived off their gardens. They put up everything, but cotton was the cash crop. They had about fifteen to twenty acres of corn, too. They ate that and fed the mules that. They ground meal for themselves; they ground chops for the chickens.

S. Wolff: What are "chops"?

J. Faulkner: Crushed corn. They made mash for corn whiskey for the whiskey stills; ear corn was for the mules. Other farmers had self-sustaining places like here. They hunted for meat. They raised meat, too, and grew vegetables, but they had to buy salt and staples, but that's about all.

In the western part of the state are the big plantations that had many slaves. The small farms had no slaves. The larger the farm got, the more hands they needed.

[Driving to Paris, a town approximately ten to twelve miles southeast of Oxford.]

F. Watkins: What can you tell us about the making of the film *Barn Burning,* which takes place in a dogtrot house?

J. Faulkner: Hal Phillips found this dogtrot house. [Pointing.] Over there they had the pot boiling, the fire burning, and where they ruined the rug.[14]

F. Watkins: Was that your own horse that you were riding in the movie?

J. Faulkner: Yes.

F. Watkins: [Whistles.] Man, did you look like Major de Spain on that horse.

J. Faulkner: My voice comes through higher on the film.

F. Watkins: That was really a striking scene, it seemed to me, Jimmy, when you loomed up to Ab Snopes's cabin.

J. Faulkner: In that scene they had poured gasoline all around that barn, and it burned pretty fast. There were just billows of flames and smoke. Most horses are scared of fire, so we had to use one of my daughter Meg's show horses because it was used to lights and sound from being in show rings. You know, I rode that horse within ten feet of that burning barn just before it went down, and it didn't bother her a bit. Just like in the show ring.

---

14. In Faulkner's story and the film version of "Barn Burning," Ab Snopes tracks mud onto the de Spains' carpet, and then, told to clean it by Major de Spain, Snopes's family ruins the rug in their cleaning process.

F. Watkins: Is this a fair question? Who decided to make you Major de Spain?

J. Faulkner: Peter Werner, I think, the director of the film.

F. Watkins: Who played Ab Snopes?

J. Faulkner: Tommy Lee Jones.

Now, this is the building in which they had the trial for Ab Snopes in *Barn Burning.* They went out and got some old desks. They had the older men dress up with the bowties and the long hair and beards. A boy from Greenwood, Shawn Whittington, played Sarty.

Anyway, they brought the wagons around here, and Sarty and Ab were in the courtroom. The blacksmith's scene was in this middle building, and they had a regular blacksmith's shop set, too. That's where they had the fight when they called Ab "barn burner." Sarty's fight with the town boys took place right here in the alley.

The conversation turns to the practice in the South during the 1800s of hiring or leasing convicts to private operations for labor. In Arkansas, Mississippi, and Louisiana, among other places, convicts built and repaired the levees that helped control flooding of the Mississippi River. Faulkner chronicles the events befalling one such convict in "Old Man." In this section Jimmy Faulkner discusses the difficulty of building a road on a levee, which helps keep this river, and others notorious for flooding, within bounds.

[En route to the nearby town of Taylor.]

J. Faulkner: Uncle Euphus[15] was a dirt contractor, and he and his crew would go into camps and build the roads and levees. They had big tents for the mules, tents and mess tents for the laborers, and they put all the black people together. They had to keep all convicts working, or they would often begin to fight. None of the prisoners ever gave his right name. One was named Jack of Diamonds; another was named Bull Dickey. I remember those two.

F. Watkins: What they'd make per day?

---

15. Jimmy's maternal second cousin.

J. Faulkner: Probably a dollar. That would buy about what twenty dollars would now. The way they would move dirt was to make a borrow pit where they would dig the dirt that would build up the levee or road bed. There would be thirty or forty teams of mules hitched to a single or double slip. They would form a circle of continuously moving mule teams with one walking driver to a team. The driver would walk off to one side of the slip with the cotton plow lines from the mule's bridle laying across his back and attached to each of his hands. One part of the circle would start down in the borrow pit with a man to hold the slip low to scoop up a full load of dirt, then go back to load the next slip in line in the never-ending circle of mule teams. The circle would lap up on the road bed or levee where another man would stand to dump each load as it came up.

My mother's cousin, Garland Kimmons,[16] who worked for a dirt-moving company owned by Uncle Euphus, carried a pistol with him all the time—but he never kept it in the same place two days in a row. He was about six feet eight inches, or something like that, and pretty tough—the John Cullen[17] type.

He supervised about thirty workers. They would have thirty, forty pairs of mules pulling slips like that, you know. Once or twice a day, he would take out his pistol, shoot at a bird, and then put the gun back in a different place. All the workers would stop their usual whistling as they worked to turn around and see where he put the gun [pointing to breast and hip pocket], either here or in his pocket. They would all stop whistling when they got close to him to figure out where the pistol was. But they never did.

F. Watkins: Now, this is building a road. Right?

J. Faulkner: Building a road or cutting a levee out.

F. Watkins: I see.

J. Faulkner: The Colonel used convict labor when he built his railroad.

16. Lucille "Dolly" Ramey Falkner's cousin-in-law.
17. Longtime hunting companion of William Faulkner and author of the book *Old Times.*

F. Watkins: He could use convict labor because he paid the state so much money in building the railroad to hire the labor.[18]

J. Faulkner: Right.

F. Watkins: And he fed them.

J. Faulkner: Fed them and paid the state so much a day.

F. Watkins: Probably just a few pennies.

J. Faulkner: Yes. He had to bring back one body—dead or alive—for each one he took out.

F. Watkins: Oh, I see.

J. Faulkner: You see, if he went down to Parchman and got a hundred laborers, he'd have to bring back a hundred, the same hundred. But they could be dead.

F. Watkins: What was his penalty if he didn't bring them back?

J. Faulkner: I don't remember.

F. Watkins: In the story "Old Man," they would use convict labor in an emergency. The Mississippi State Penitentiary was at Parchman. How many acres in the state penitentiary, Jimmy?

J. Faulkner: Twenty or thirty thousand acres in the state penitentiary, and all the convicts—who are not penned up—work that whole farm.

F. Watkins: That's right. See the water snake?

J. Faulkner: He's a multicolored one. You can tell it's a multicolored one when it opens its mouth. It looks like a ball of cotton.

F. Watkins: Now, all those convicts in "Old Man," they took the convicts and made them work on the levee while the river was flooding.

---

18. Under Mississippi's convict-lease system, the state gave complete control over the entire penal system to private contractors. Although Mississippi's state constitution was amended in 1890 to prohibit the convict-lease system, the state penitentiary board of control continued to lease out convict labor to plantation owners until 1906, when the legislature abolished such lease arrangements and established the state farm system.

Convict labor was principally used to build railroads and repair and construct levees. In the absence of state supervision of private contractors under Mississippi's lease system, convict laborers often worked under harsh and sometimes dangerous conditions. See Mark T. Coleman, *Politics and Punishment: The History of the Louisiana State Penal System* (Baton Rouge, 1971), 83; Albert Dennis Kirwan, *Revolt of the Rednecks: Mississippi Politics, 1876–1925* (Gloucester, Mass., 1964), 174–75; and *The Encyclopedia of Southern History*, ed. Roller and Twyman, 294.

J. Faulkner: Sandbagging it.

F. Watkins: Do you have a convict labor camp in this county?

J. Faulkner: No.

F. Watkins: Used to? Did you? Or not?

J. Faulkner: I'm sure the county did, but the nearest one I can remember is over close to Crenshaw.

F. Watkins: That was not in this county?

J. Faulkner: No. Next county over. If I had to guess, I'd say right about there this river is ten feet, fifteen feet deep.

F. Watkins: Oh, that much?

J. Faulkner: Yes.

F. Watkins: Would this dirt have come right out of the bottom of where this river is?

J. Faulkner: You mean the dirt to build it?

F. Watkins: This road is above the bottom.

J. Faulkner: Oh, yes, yes.

F. Watkins: Well, then, up this way they would have another hill for more dirt, right?

J. Faulkner: Right. This is a new road; it used to be low, and it flooded, and you just couldn't come across this road during high water.

F. Watkins: When I came over in the fifties, this road was paved at the time.

[Traveling about four or five miles north of Oxford around Dead Man's Curve.]

J. Faulkner: Now, Tula's in the southeast part of the county. Taylor's in the southwest part. Dead Man's Curve is just north of Oxford on Highway 7. Dead Man's Curve was like the place in *Flags in the Dust* where Old Bayard had a heart attack and died in the car when Young Bayard was racing his car around the county. The first time I ever heard of anybody killed in a car wreck was on that curve. It was on Dead Man's Curve.

F. Watkins: Old Bayard Sartoris of *The Unvanquished* was the only Sartoris who died a nonviolent death. He died in the novel *Sartoris* or *Flags in the Dust,* which was published about nine years before *The*

Unvanquished. I think that Faulkner let him die of a heart attack because he was the one that in Reconstruction restored peace to Yoknapatawpha County, after the violence of Reconstruction.

But young Bayard came home from World War I much disturbed and driving as wild as one or two of those cars that went by our picnic. He got his grandfather in the car with him, and they were going around on an old road at Dead Man's Curve. But instead of driving around the curve, he just went straight across it. When he got across, he realized that in the fright his grandfather died of a heart attack.

So he wandered way out into the country for several days during Christmas; he then left the county—after he'd eaten a meal and spent the night at a black man's home—and went on to Memphis ultimately and was killed as a test pilot in a plane that everybody knew he could not fly. We're going around that curve, now.

TAYLOR

She looked about, at the bleak yellow station, the overalled men chewing slowly and watching her, down the track at the diminishing train, at the four puffs of vapor that had almost died away when the sound of the whistle came back.

—*Sanctuary*

Taylor, a town several miles to the southwest of Oxford, figures in Faulkner's novel Sanctuary. *The train tracks are no longer visible in Taylor, and the depot no longer exists.*

J. Faulkner: The fictional Old Frenchman's Place might have been located about four miles right over yonder south of here in Taylor.[19]

F. Watkins: Was there a Grenier who lived down in here some place? That was an invented name, wasn't it?

J. Faulkner: That could be. Taylor was a big town at one time.

F. Watkins: Had seventeen saloons.

J. Faulkner: Yes. It was a tough town, too. A lot of these little towns, hell, they weren't little towns—they were about the size of Oxford. It just happened that Oxford had the courthouse.

19. Louis Grenier's plantation.

Fig. 33. Taylor grocery and restaurant. At the depot in the town of Taylor, Temple Drake emerges from the train in *Sanctuary*. (*Photograph by Billy Howard*)

F. Watkins: Now, Taylor was the place where Temple got off the train.[20]

J. Faulkner: That house by the railroad track here in Taylor was a whorehouse at one time.

F. Watkins: But not like Miss Reba's in Memphis. That was a city whorehouse.

J. Faulkner: The train station used to be right in here someplace.

F. Watkins: Wasn't Taylor founded at the same time as Oxford?

J. Faulkner: Yes.

F. Watkins: As I recall, all the land was taken in 1832 or so in the Treaty of Pontotoc. It used to be a thriving place until they tore the schoolhouse down.

J. Faulkner: Any little town, you know, that had a schoolhouse and a post office was in pretty fair shape. But they consolidated the schools about 1954–55, and they tore this one down. There used to be a

20. See William Faulkner's *Sanctuary*.

row of houses just like that house there, up and down the railroad track, where the people who worked around here roomed and boarded.

Uncle John Markette was a conductor on the railroad.[21] He got mad at Taylor one time. He came through Taylor—his run was from Water Valley to Holly Springs—running his train about seventy miles an hour, and the town men jumped on him about it. So the next day he stopped down in town and tied a rope to the front of the train, started pulling on the rope, and got the engineer to run the train real slow. He walked through town like he was pulling the train. [Laughter.]

F. Watkins: So that was an old boardinghouse over there. Was it ever used for any other purpose, Jimmy?

J. Faulkner: It was a whorehouse at one time, a thriving one.

F. Watkins: That ex-boardinghouse—that wouldn't be over eighty years old, would it?

J. Faulkner: I would guess around eighty or a hundred.

F. Watkins: Do you know if the town of Taylor was named after a particular person?

J. Faulkner: Just the Taylor family.

F. Watkins: No famous people?

J. Faulkner: No.

F. Watkins: What would be the population of this town now, Jimmy?

J. Faulkner: It's got down to around three hundred. They just reincorporated.

F. Watkins: We just passed a house like the one in which Ab Snopes in *The Hamlet* met up with Pat Stamper and lost his cream separator.

That's the geography of it, but Faulkner created the fiction out of his imagination in conjunction with the hundreds of people he knew.

J. Faulkner: Things were happening back then, you know—the railroad company was the big money-maker. When somebody needed money, they'd get an old mule and tie it on the railroad. The train would

---

21. See Blotner, *Faulkner: A Biography*, I, 488, for further details.

hit it, and they'd collect money for the mule. That was a fairly common thing.[22]

F. Watkins: Have all the Taylors died out?

J. Faulkner: No. The old man's grandson is still alive in Memphis. He's a lawyer and almost blind now. He's not very old.

F. Watkins: Look at that old outhouse!

[Passing Wyatt's Crossing in the former town of Wyatt.]

J. Faulkner: This is Wyatt's Crossing, about ten miles northwest of Oxford on the Tallahatchie River. Wyatt's Crossing at one time—well, in the late 1850s—was vying with Memphis for trade on the river because they shipped a lot of cotton from up at Wyatt like they did at Memphis. But when Sherman came through, he burned it, and it was never built back. There were two or three taverns left over there.

Old Chief Toby Tubby was a rich old Indian. He had just sold—I forgot how many thousands of acres of land. I don't want to tie myself down to a certain time—a month, two months, three months prior to going over to Wyatt. Anyway, he went into a saloon over there and got drunk. He got into a fight and was killed. They supposedly buried him with his money. He also had a slave, and they were going bury this slave alive with him. [Bird call.] Of course, some white folks got together and stopped that.[23]

F. Watkins: When was this, Jimmy?

J. Faulkner: Around 1840.

F. Watkins: He was a Chickasaw?

J. Faulkner: Yes. Later on, his daughter came down, and she hired some people to go around his grave and dig, hunting that treasure. She had hired ten or twelve to dig, and they dug for about a week.

Then one afternoon she fired them. The next day she was gone—they went out there and found the imprint in the ground of boxes and

22. See William Faulkner's story "Mule in the Yard."

23. For a story about such a live burial, see Faulkner's story "Red Leaves." See also Floyd C. Watkins, "Sacrificial Rituals and Anguish in the Victim's Heart in 'Red Leaves,'" *Studies in Short Fiction,* XXX (Winter, 1993).

kettles. She left this part of the country, and nobody ever heard from her.[24]

F. Watkins: Where did you hear this story?

J. Faulkner: I'm not sure; it's one that I grew up with; I don't quite know where or when I heard it.

F. Watkins: You heard it a lot of times?

J. Faulkner: Yes. Well, Lucius Coleman—did you ever know Lucius?

F. Watkins: Never did.

J. Faulkner: He got put in jail every Saturday night. When I'd go by the jail, he'd yell at me to help get him out of jail. Well, Lucius spent his entire life digging at Toby Tubby's grave, but he never did find any gold.

F. Watkins: Are you aware of the parallel between Lucius Beauchamp in "The Fire and the Hearth" and the digging?

J. Faulkner: Yes, some of it.

F. Watkins: Digging in a grave or an Indian mound?

J. Faulkner: Yes.

F. Watkins: Do you think that William himself had heard that story?

J. Faulkner: Oh, yes. Lord, yes.

F. Watkins: I don't know any scholar who has written that, do you?

J. Faulkner: No. Lucius worked for everybody around town.

F. Watkins: Which is the road to Memphis, say, during *The Reivers?*

J. Faulkner: We're standing on it. We are about six miles northwest of Oxford.

F. Watkins: Is this the old road to Memphis?

J. Faulkner: Yes, it was until 1930—well, I take that back. It was destroyed as a road when they built the reservoir in 1937.

F. Watkins: So, actually, the road to Memphis, where you go out north of the square as it is now, did not figure as the road to Memphis in very many of Faulkner's works at all.

24. See Faulkner, *Requiem for a Nun.* See also Blotner, *Faulkner: A Biography,* I, 72–73.

J. Faulkner: Not too much. Now, when I was little, we would go to Memphis that way because we would get on better roads at Holly Springs. Now, this was a gravel road—no, it wasn't—a dirt road. But I had been this way; it's shorter because Memphis is northwest of Oxford.

Old Oxford Plantations

Frenchman's Bend was a section of rich river-bottom country lying twenty miles southeast of Jefferson. Hill cradled and remote, definite yet without boundaries, straddling into two counties and owning allegiance to neither, it had been the original grant and site of a tremendous pre–Civil War plantation, the ruins of which—the gutted shell of an enormous house with its fallen stables and slave quarters and overgrown gardens and brick terraces and promenades—were still known as the Old Frenchman's place, although the original boundaries now existed only on old faded records in the Chancery Clerk's office in the county court house in Jefferson, and even some of the once fertile fields had long since reverted to the cane and cypress jungle from which their first master had hewed them.

—*The Hamlet*

The Jones, Pettis, Shipp, and Pegues plantations were four of the largest and most profitable farms owned by some of the first settlers in the Lafayette County. These plantations resemble in scope the land and home that was Thomas Sutpen's in Absalom, Absalom! *Although courthouse records indicate that no one individual in Lafayette County held title to one hundred square miles of land, as Sutpen did in the fictional account, the land grants of several large landowners equaled the breadth of Sutpen's ownership. H. A. Barr, Goodloe W. Buford, Alexander Pegues, and W. D. Pettis were among these large landowners in the northwest part of the county. The Pettis plantation house has burned down, but a drive through the county on this property, now returned to forest, gives a feeling of the transitory nature of land ownership and the spoils of modernity—two common Faulkner themes made almost palpable by the immediate landscape. Jimmy's talk about the varied legends surrounding these large landowners suggests that Faulkner may have drawn his portrait of the man named Sutpen, as well as the families of McCaslin and McCallum in* Absalom, Absalom!; Go Down, Moses; *and* Sartoris, *from the Pettis brothers and their families, collectively.*

The Pettis Plantation

J. Faulkner: In my mind this is the Pettis place, was and is still. It's government land now, taken by the government for the reservoir.

We are riding through the part of the county Sutpen's Hundred is most likely based on. Right behind that house, which is about a half mile north of College Hill, is Hedleston Lake. When Brother Will was a scout leader, he took his scouts over there and camped. Nanny and Big Dad used to take me over there when Brother Will was scoutmaster, and I'd stay a while and swim with them. But because I was so little, they'd take me back to town at night.

Brother Will knew this area well, and he hunted here with Lucky, Benno, and Walter Pettis; Will Lewis; and all that bunch. Anyway, they were the real hunters around here. Lucky was the best rifle shot, and Benno was the best shotgun shot.

F. Watkins: How many of those Pettis brothers were there?

J. Faulkner: Four, I think.

F. Watkins: All of them married?

J. Faulkner: One married.

F. Watkins: Could they be one of the sources for the McCallums in *Sartoris?*

J. Faulkner: I don't know. I think Walter was the prototype for Walter Ewell in *Go Down, Moses.*

F. Watkins: Walter Pettis was his actual name?

J. Faulkner: I think.

F. Watkins: I've hunted with one of the Pettis brothers—Lucky Pettis.

J. Faulkner: That's his brother.

F. Watkins: Lucky wrote some poems and carried them to William one time. Did you know that?

J. Faulkner: No, I didn't.

F. Watkins: He knew somebody in New York that offered to publish them, but William read them and said, "No. Don't put up the money."

J. Faulkner: The last three of those brothers who were living together—Walter, Lucky, and Benno—lived in a big room in the wintertime and kept the fire going all night to keep warm. They got mad at Walter one time about something, so they put him in the corner of the room and wouldn't let him come out into the rest of the room. He was sixty-seven years old at the time.

F. Watkins: You once said there was a large grant up here of almost a hundred square miles. To what family?

J. Faulkner: Pettis.

F. Watkins: But the only sure parallel to Sutpen we know is the amount of land they owned—almost a hundred square miles? Has that been checked on the deed books of the Pettis family, or anything?[25]

J. Faulkner: No, I've just been told that.

F. Watkins: Did the Pettises tell you that?

J. Faulkner: No, I don't know who did. But I do know that their farm went from over here, past Highway 6, towards Batesville. I do know that they had about three hundred families on it.

F. Watkins: You know that?

J. Faulkner: I *know* that. Pettis had almost one hundred sections of land back then, and they had about three hundred families living on it. Thomas Sutpen lived close enough to get to church, where he met Ellen Coldfield. Right here on this ridge is the hollow where one of the two enormous Pettis houses sat; the other one sat on the other ridge, and they could call to each other across the hollow. The land went from back

25. Court records and studies of Lafayette County history indicate that great activity occurred between 1830 and 1839 among "speculators who wanted to buy land and Indians who wanted to sell." In fact, "there were land sales almost every day. . . . Among the earliest purchasers of land in that part of the Chickasaw Cession which is now included within the present county of Lafayette were the following men: Goodlow W. Buford, Joseph Caruthers, John P. Jones, Malichi Pegues [among others]." These men "had their deeds recorded during 1836 and the early months of 1837. . . . By the middle of 1837, [Joseph Caruthers] had purchased the large acreage of thirty and one-half sections of land. The total cost of this land was $36,900." By 1850 two men owned five thousand acres apiece—Washington Price and Thomas Fondran—but by 1860 only A. H. Pegues owned five thousand acres. Four men owned as much as three thousand acres; they were W. T. Pettus, W. T. Isom, E. W. Price, and Z. Kilgore (John Cooper Hathorn, *Early Settlers of Lafayette Co., Mississippi: A Period of Study of Lafayette County, from 1836–1860, with Emphasis on Population Groups* [Oxford, Miss., 1980], 4, 5, 48–53).

this way—I don't know how far back in there—all the way across Highway 6. There was also a family cemetery on the land between them which they used for both themselves and their slaves.

Now, Old Man Ben, Benno Pettis' father, just died about twenty, twenty-five years ago. We saw Pettis' tombstone at the cemetery behind the church.

[Driving for miles.]

J. Faulkner: This land is another part of the old Pettis place; this is one of the old barns.

F. Watkins: What kind of home would they have had up there?

J. Faulkner: It was a plantation-type home, sitting up on top of a hill.

F. Watkins: Like yours?

J. Faulkner: No, one story put up on stilts.

F. Watkins: I saw a dogtrot house here in the sixties that had columns running up to the second floor when they didn't have anything but the roof on the second floor.

J. Faulkner: Both of the Pettis houses burned, and there's nothing left. The fire started right here.

F. Watkins: That's where the source for the Sutpen plantation most likely was?

J. Faulkner: Right. The Pettises had slaves, then, and they were given the last name Pettis; he put names on the graves. One of the Pettis girls married a Frierson. Their son, Red Frierson, used to strip down to the waist when he worked. He looked just about like Thomas Sutpen, I guess. He used to wrestle cows that had gone wild down in the bottom and bring them in all by himself to sell.

F. Watkins: Except for the big homes, I haven't seen the old, small country homes. They may have just been burned or torn down in the last ten years [1970–80].

J. Faulkner: Yes. They weren't built strong enough; they were built out of green lumber. Some just rotted out, but more were torn down.

[Driving for miles.]

J. Faulkner: This is still the old Pettis place. This is it!

F. Watkins: Back where we were standing, too?

J. Faulkner: Yes. We're still on it! It stretches for miles.

F. Watkins: We are still on it.

J. Faulkner: They've changed this road a little bit on me, now. That dirt road went back up to one of the plantation houses, one of the old Pettis houses. The Pettis place begins in the northwest corner of the county, two or three miles from College Hill.

F. Watkins: Why do you think Wash Jones's[26] cabin was here?

J. Faulkner: In my mind the Wash Jones cabin was out in here. This would have been it. Right in that meadow over yonder. We're still on old Pettis' place, but, back in 1936 or 1937, or thereabouts, the government bought all land beneath a certain contour line for the Sardis Reservoir. This is the Sardis Reservoir. The Tallahatchie River was dammed up. In my mind I've always thought that the Wash Jones cabin was right here on Brother Will's map because it was a fishing camp. This is where they fished on the Tallahatchie River. The channel of the Tallahatchie River is not too far out in there.

Jones would have built a cabin high enough to be away from a flood. The old Pettis house is not too far up that way, which I think corresponds to where the Sutpen house would have been. That's why I think that Wash Jones's cabin was in an area like this one: he could ride down to the fishing camp.

F. Watkins: You don't know what the Sutpen-Coldfield marriage was based on, do you?

J. Faulkner: No, I don't.

F. Watkins: So there's nothing wrong with the story if Faulkner completely invented it. As far as you know, the story of Sutpen's daughter making the horses run wild to church might have come completely out of William Faulkner's head.

---

26. See Faulkner, *Absalom, Absalom!*

J. Faulkner: Right. But, you know, any fiction has some basis of some truth.

The Jones Plantation

It was dark among the cedars, the light more dark than gray even, the quiet rain, the faint pearly globules, materializing on the gun barrels and the five headstones like drops of not quite congealed meltings from cold candles on the marble: the two flat heavy vaulted slabs, the other three headstones leaning a little awry, with here and there a carved letter or even an entire word momentary and legible in the faint light which the raindrops brought particle by particle into the gloom and released.

—*Absalom, Absalom!*

The Jones plantation, or as some refer to it, the Old Jones Place, was purchased by William J. Jones in 1836 from the Native American Wee Hun Na Yo.[27] The home Jones built, circa 1838–40,[28] was once known for the intricately carved cypress woodwork of its staircases, baseboards, panels, windows, and doors. Houses like the Jones place, the Pettis plantation, and the Shipp home most likely informed the portrait of Sutpen's home and land. The small family cemetery behind the house resembles that which captured Faulkner's imagination in Absalom, Absalom! *Each year, visitors and townsfolk witnessed the decay of these homes. In 1995, the home is no longer standing.*

[Several miles southeast of Taylor.]

F. Watkins: When we went to the Old Jones Place last time, we didn't even go into the old house. You think we ought to keep out of the house this time?

J. Faulkner: I expect so. That thing is about to fall in. Last time I saw it—well, you were here—it was about to fall down.

F. Watkins: The Shipp house burned?

---

27. Lafayette County Courthouse, *Sectional Index to Lands in Lafayette County, Mississippi. Sections 1–36, Township 9-South, Range 4-West,* XXII (Oxford, Miss.: n.d.).

28. According to the mayor of Taylor, Mississippi, Jane Rule Burdine, who spoke with a relative of the Jones family, the house was built between 1838 and 1840.

J. Faulkner: Right. The Shipp house burned.[29]

S. Wolff: Where do you locate the home most like the Old Frenchman's Place?

J. Faulkner: I think the Shipp house was closer to the model for the Frenchman's Place. It looked like Rowan Oak does now. The Jones plantation was really a model of the location for Sutpen's land. The Shipp home was more a model for the home itself. Brother Will was thinking of Yoknapatawpha but not seeing just one home. The county had quite a few of them.

F. Watkins: Well, I believe this is as close to what the Old Frenchman's Place was modeled on as the Shipp house was.

J. Faulkner: It's as close in distance. They're two miles apart.

F. Watkins: Right. That was a lot more magnificent house than the Jones place.

S. Wolff: Frenchman's Bend is a real name, isn't it?

J. Faulkner: Yes, it's an area out near Tula. It's a bend in the river known as the place where Indians were killed. Brother Will made the name into a town. We went to Tula in April and saw that old wooden house with the scalloped wooden balustrade and the beehives around it.

29. Dr. Felix Grundy Shipp, one of the earliest of the Shipp family to come from Tennessee, moved to Water Valley, located in the northern part of Mississippi, in 1833. After building an inn, Dr. Shipp began construction on his plantation. The plantation succeeded so well that Dr. Shipp began building his mansion in 1856. The bricks used for the foundation and the chimney were handmade from the clay taken from "the red hills." The house was framed by huge timbers that were notched and pegged together. The cypress shingles were hand split and dipped in linseed oil for long-lasting protection. The mansion contained a medicine room that Dr. Shipp used to store and dispense homemade medicines concocted from recipes written in a small leather-bound journal. The quarterly Methodist conferences were also held at the Shipp mansion.

In 1862, during the Civil War, Dr. Shipp left Mississippi to avoid General Grant and his Union soldiers. The Shipp women and slaves tried to hide the food and livestock to prevent the Union soldiers from discovering them. Unfortunately, the Union soldiers broke in and confiscated what they wanted.

By 1918 all the Shipp family members had left the mansion, and the house was "rented to tenants who had no respect at all" for the place. In the early 1970s the mansion burned down, and today only the grand cedar trees and the Shipp cemetery remain. See *Heritage of Lafayette County, Mississippi* (Dallas, Tex., 1986), I, 550; Blotner, *Faulkner: A Biography,* I, 889–90; and Marshall, "Scenes from Yoknapatawpha," 197–200.

Fig. 34. The Jones plantation, here with punched-out windows filled in by bed clothing, once had beautiful cypress woodwork in its baseboards and staircases. The owner would not sell until some years after the floors had fallen in. (*Courtesy of the Floyd C. Watkins Collection, Special Collections Department, Robert W. Woodruff Library, Emory University*)

I have put that house in my mind as a possible model for the Old Frenchman's Place, too. Brother Will talked about the Old Frenchman's Place as the place where Stevens took Temple Drake.

S. Wolff: How do you locate the Old Frenchman's Place?

J. Faulkner: Temple got off the train in Taylor, so the Shipp house might be closer in location to the Old Frenchman's Place. The Shipp house is sort of in the middle of the southern part of the county. Old Dr. Shipp built it. The Shipp house may have burned by grass fire, maybe lightning; it just happens sometime.

[Pointing to an old barn.] Now, here's one of those old barns falling down there, back up in there. You could get a house in that barn.

J. Faulkner: Now, the old Jones house is still standing, but barely.

F. Watkins: There's no driveway up to there, is there? Now, here's a one-lane bridge—one of them. See how the boards run parallel to the road for the wagon wheels to run on.

Fig. 35. Another view of the Jones plantation home (*Courtesy of the Floyd C. Watkins Collection, Special Collections Department, Robert W. Woodruff Library, Emory University*)

Fig. 36. The Shipp plantation home, *ca.* 1957. The home burned in the late 1950s. (*Courtesy of the Floyd C. Watkins Collection, Special Collections Department, Robert W. Woodruff Library, Emory University*)

Fig. 37. Shipp home, front view with cedars. (Courtesy of the Floyd C. Watkins Collection, Special Collections Department, Robert W. Woodruff Library, Emory University)

Fig. 38. The Shipp family cemetery, *ca.* 1958. Compare with the Sutpen cemetery in *Absalom, Absalom!* (*Courtesy of the Floyd C. Watkins Collection, Special Collections Department, Robert W. Woodruff Library, Emory University*)

Is this a treacherous stream?

J. Faulkner: Yes. It floods.

F. Watkins: Except for this Jones plantation house, there weren't really a lot of pre–Civil War plantation houses out in the county, were there?

J. Faulkner: Not this way.

F. Watkins: Were there any in the northern part of the county?

J. Faulkner: College Hill was full of them. They had, I guess, fifteen or twenty out there.

F. Watkins: How many are left?

J. Faulkner: None. They all burned or something happened to them.

F. Watkins: Every one of them?

J. Faulkner: Yes.

Fig. 39. An old grave in Lafayette County like the graves Faulkner describes in Yoknapatawpha (*Courtesy of the Floyd C. Watkins Collection, Special Collections Department, Robert W. Woodruff Library, Emory University*)

Fig. 40. A large, wooden farmhouse near Tula, Mississippi. This style of house, now almost extinct, is likely the kind of house Faulkner wrote about in *The Hamlet* and other works. (*Photograph by Billy Howard*)

[Approaching the Old Jones Place, a home still standing but in ruins.]

There's also a problem with snakes around this building. The Jones house has deteriorated in the last two years since you've been here. You see that wall leaning back in there? That'll be gone the next time you are here. Don't get too close to the house. See how it is tilting backwards now? It'll go down one of these days soon.

F. Watkins: Now, this house has homemade square nails and slave-made bricks from the 1840s or 1850s?

J. Faulkner: Yes.

F. Watkins: There is such unbelievably rich woodwork in this house: baseboards made out of cypress; staircases—marvelous woodwork. Do you know what price the owner was offered recently for this house?

J. Faulkner: I don't know.

F. Watkins: It's rumored to have been an enormously high price for the woodwork. Now, you couldn't even get in to get it without the risk of the house falling on you. For a long time the current owner refused to sell the woodwork. He wanted to keep it, but he didn't want to let it rot, either. That man wouldn't sell that wonderful woodwork. What he didn't know was that you can't keep things without preserving them somehow.

Jimmy, you said this house is one of the poorer plantation homes because it has a balustrade?

J. Faulkner: Yes.

F. Watkins: It has only a wooden rather than an ornate, iron balustrade. I don't believe that anywhere in Lafayette County you would find a balustrade like the elaborate ones in New Orleans. Would you have found a big, iron balustrade on the Pegues home, or do you remember?

J. Faulkner: They didn't have one on that house.

F. Watkins: Not one at all?

J. Faulkner: No. Now, in the eighteenth century, houses like this had shutters but no screens. They did have mosquito netting.

F. Watkins: I see.

J. Faulkner: All of these nails are square, too. You might be able to find some, but you'll have to dig them up.

F. Watkins: Some people have used metal detectors. You might even find gold around here.

J. Faulkner: I've been over the ground at my own house a little. Dr. Cook, of the History Department at Ole Miss, is a Civil War buff, and he comes out to my house, too. He has found many relics. He's shown me heel taps off Federal boots. He has found cans, pieces of cans, and food cans that he claims were Federal because the Federal troops occupied this area for a while and took supplies. They camped around my house—yard, really. Sherman's troops did.

This is the Jones family cemetery.

S. Wolff: The family had its own small cemetery near the house. Faulkner describes a family cemetery fictionally in *Absalom, Absalom!*

Fig. 41. A one-lane wooden bridge in Lafayette County. On a similar bridge the wagon and wild horses collide in "Spotted Horses." (*Photograph by Billy Howard*)

[En route to the next farm.]

F. Watkins: Is that a modern barn?

J. Faulkner: Yes. Made of logs. Well, I'm sorry. I'm afraid that little wooden bridge you saw in 1957 is gone. It was right here.

THE JOE PARKS FARM

The last stop is a former residence of the Faulkner family and the home of Joe Parks, an Oxford citizen and one of many possible sources for the Flem Snopes portrait.

J. Faulkner: This is the farm[30] right here where we lived back in the 1930s; we raised mules across the creek down there. The commissary was set right here behind that old dead tree. Old Man Joe Parks lived in

30. Greenfield Farm.

that house before he moved to town and got hold of the First National Bank.[31] There's a little house sitting on just the other side there. Brother Will would go there and write for a few days at a time when he needed to get away from the town and people.

F. Watkins: Well, the house is still here, but you can't see it.

J. Faulkner: Yes.

F. Watkins: I came out here once when a worker named Renzi was there. What was his last name?

J. Faulkner: McJunkin. Renzi was about the toughest fellow out here. He was about six feet six inches and weighed about two hundred and twenty pounds in good shape. James[32] is a quarter Indian, and he can handle a knife better than anybody; I got him out of jail one time because he'd cut a fellow's ear off. I asked him how come, and he said, "He just stepped too close to my knife." Well, Renzi and James went off one Sunday to a funeral, and they both got drunk on home brew. They were back up here some place in the cemetery, and they had to dig a grave. They lowered the coffin in the grave, and Renzi fell into the grave with the coffin. James said he came up cold sober.

F. Watkins: How far are we from Oxford?

J. Faulkner: Seventeen miles. Memphis to Vicksburg is two hundred and fifty miles, if I'm not mistaken. That's from point to point.

31. A one-time stockholder in the First National Bank of Oxford, Joe Parks eventually ousted then-president John Wesley Thompson Falkner, the Young Colonel, and became president himself. These events loosely parallel Flem Snope's rise to power. See Blotner, *Faulkner: A Biography,* I, 257–60; and Marshall, "Scenes from Yoknapatawpha," 191.

32. James Avant.

4

MISS PEARLE AND MOTEE:
ACQUAINTANCES OF WILLIAM FAULKNER

The store in which the Justice of the Peace's court was sitting smelled of cheese. The boy, crouched on his nail keg at the back of the crowded room, knew he smelled cheese, and more: from where he sat he could see the ranked shelves close-packed with the solid, squat, dynamic shapes of tin cans whose labels his stomach read, not from the lettering which meant nothing to his mind but from the scarlet devils and the silver curve of fish—this, the cheese which he knew he smelled and the hermetic meat which his intestines believed he smelled coming in intermittent gusts momentary and brief between the other constant one, the smell and sense just a little of fear because mostly of despair and grief, the old fierce pull of blood.

—"Barn Burning"

In this chapter the interviewers meet two now-elderly acquaintances of William Faulkner: Pearle Galloway and Motee Daniel. Their talk demonstrates how easily Faulkner would have come upon the raw material of his fiction just by speaking to his neighbors. The first visit is with Miss Pearle Galloway, a native of Oxford, Mississippi. She inherited one of the oldest businesses in the county, a general store. Like her father before her, Miss Pearle kept her store well stocked with hoop cheese, sardines, candy, baking supplies—flour, sugar, and salt—and even farm equipment. Although no particular character in Faulkner represents Miss Pearle, she is an archetype of characters Faulkner wrote about.

Miss Pearle's stories about Faulkner depict him as a generous man who assisted with the commodities food program, yet also as a reserved, abrupt individual who rarely spoke to people he passed on the street. Her recollections are nostalgic for the simpler times in the Oxford of Faulkner's era.

During the interview Miss Pearle shows the interviewers a land grant in her possession. It deeds land to a Native American chief, Noosakahtubby. Signed by Martin Van Buren, the grant is typical of land exchanges between Native Americans and Anglo-Europeans at the time of the Civil War and before. Such transactions, of much interest to Faulkner, form the basis for stories such as "The Old People," "The Bear," and "Red Leaves."

Miss Pearle and Her Store

A small, wooden building houses Pearle Galloway's store. This style of building is called a shotgun because the rooms link in a row from front to back as if a single shotgun blast would go straight through them. Although open at the time of the interview, the store is now closed.

J. Faulkner: This is the store where *Intruder in The Dust* was filmed. Come in and meet Miss Pearle. Miss Pearle has closed her store, but she's opened it today just for us to see it. Miss Pearle, there probably won't be another group of visitors that will get to see the store before you sell it.

F. Watkins: Hello, Miss Pearle. Do you remember me?

P. Galloway: I remember that you've been here before.

F. Watkins: How old is the store, Jimmy?

J. Faulkner: I think it's the first one in Lafayette County.

F. Watkins: These are the original boards on the front of the store. Were the logs sawed by slaves?

P. Galloway: Yes.

F. Watkins: I'm sorry you're getting rid of the store.

P. Galloway: Well, I'm not getting rid of it, I am—well—it's not of my choosing. I'm being forced out.

F. Watkins: I'm sorry to hear that. Miss Pearle, we brought a ham. Can we use your old cheese cutter to cut that ham up with? We'd like to talk history with you as we eat our lunch.

P. Galloway: That cheese cutter is over at my house. I have a knife you can use. I have been robbed many times, and I have been frightened beyond words. My family and my doctor told me to get out of it, said you cannot live this way. For two weeks my sister-in-law and I stayed here with a gun in a pocket.

F. Watkins: When was the first time you were robbed?

P. Galloway: Last fall a young person came in, and I thought he had a gun. He held it on me and said, "Give me your money." I said, "What are you talking about?" And he says, "Give me your money." I had a stick about this long, a seasoned oak stick under the counter, and I pulled it out and reared it back. I said, "You get out of here." [Extreme laughter.] He ran.

F. Watkins: You mean from the 1920s until 1979 there was never an attempt to rob this store?

P. Galloway: Oh, somebody had broken in a few times, but they didn't walk in and take it away. It's the times. The people don't have much respect for you, your life, or anything else.

F. Watkins: Were these robbers local people or people from far off?

P. Galloway: I don't know how far off; they would always walk. It was always a different one, and he would always grab what he could and run right out across there. The robber would always wait till there was nobody here but me. [Sound of quail calling.] Later I talked my sister-in-law into coming over and staying with me for about two months. I thought they wouldn't bother two people, but they did.

I don't know if you know about the old store. These windows here, the shutters opened. There is a glass window on the inside; I had this thing fastened to each side, and it opened one day when we had a high wind. It knocked it open, split one side of it, and I asked the carpenter if he could fix that split. He said, "I'll just go to town and get some new lumber. That's the only way to fix it," and I said, "No, you don't, what else can you do?" He said, "Nail it up." I said, "Nail it up." It's nailed up.

Fig. 42. Pearle Galloway's store in College Hill, Mississippi
(*Photograph by Billy Howard*)

S. Wolff: Miss Pearle, may we look at your land grant?

P. Galloway: Yes, I have it framed.

[Miss Pearle displays the framed document signed by President Martin
    Van Buren granting land to a Native American chief.][1]

S. Wolff: I'm reading from the grant now. The land grant is to an
Indian named Noosakahtubby and reads: "Land ceded to the U.S. by the
treaty concluded at Pontotoc Creek 20 October 1832, with the Chickasaw Nation. Two sections, 25 January 1863 . . . 1221 acres and 76 hun-
dredths of an acre in the district of Sands . . . Subject to sale at Pontotoc,
Mississippi." The grant is signed by Martin Van Buren.

P. Galloway: Noosakahtubby was an Indian chief.

S. Wolff: Who gave the official paper to your daddy?

1. For years Miss Pearle displayed the land grant in her store.

P. Galloway: Mr. Buford—Mr. Robby Buford.[2] His daddy was John Aubrey Buford. His uncle, Tubby Buford, was a friend of the Indian who lived on Goose Creek and a friend of Toby Tubby. There is a story that Tubby Buford followed the Indian around and knew where he hid his money—somewhere on the creek bank.

F. Watkins: Tubby meant chief. When did your family get this store?

P. Galloway: Sometime in the late 1920s, I guess. Mr. Buford, whose ancestors were early settlers here, was a great friend of my dad's. He was the one who gave the land grant document to him.

F. Watkins: I see. How did you spell "Buford"?

P. Galloway: B-u-f-o-r-d.

F. Watkins: It's sometimes B-e-a-u-f-o-r-t. That was called "Buford."

P. Galloway: Well, they spell it B-u-f-o-r-d: Buford.

J. Faulkner: Someone started calling Lucas Beauchamp "Beecham." Nanny asked Brother Will how do you pronounce it, and he said, "Just like it sounds, 'Bow-Champ.' "

S. Wolff: Will you tell us more about your store?

P. Galloway: Well, College Hill Church was organized in 1836. The church building was not completed until '44, and this was one of the first stores built, so I'm supposing that somewhere during that period of time the store was built. You know, when the people came in here to settle, there was no place to go to buy except here. They had silk dresses, gold watches, and all that kind of thing in here then. I have tried to get a record of all the people who have owned this store, but I waited till some of the elderly people had gotten where they didn't remember, you know—like me. So I missed a lot of it. You know, the early ones. I have lived here all of my life, and it means a lot to me because I'm a native of College Hill.

At one time this was the post office—this store is where we got our mail—where we mailed letters. I still have some pictures of the store to sell. Twenty-five cents.

2. A common name in Oxford, "Buford" appears in Faulkner's *Light in August* as the name of a Jefferson deputy sheriff.

F. Watkins: May we have some?

P. Galloway: Thank you very much.

F. Watkins: Do your drink bottles require a deposit?

P. Galloway: You can throw away the orange juice containers, but not the Coca-Cola bottles.

F. Watkins: We're bringing in some crackers now; do you happen to have crackers to sell?

P. Galloway: Yes, sir. But if you have some, just bring 'em in.

F. Watkins: Well, we can use these later. We didn't know. So we'll buy crackers from you.

P. Galloway: No, you won't. No, you don't have to do that. You know what? I had a man come back after he had worked for the county and been in here getting lunches every week for years and years; he got another job, and he came back to see me before I got out of the business. He said, "You know what? I feel like I can come in here when I get ready to do what I want to." He said, "I have been in here many a day, brought my lunch, and set back here by your heater and eaten it and you treated me just like I had bought it here."

F. Watkins: So you don't mind?

P. Galloway: No, I don't.

F. Watkins: All right. Well, we've bought crackers from you every time before.

P. Galloway: Well, that's all right. That's all right. I hope you'll come back to see me even though I'm not in business.

[At the door.]

F. Watkins: All right. We'll run up and look at the old store from the outside two years from now. Look at that brick; it has *Oxford* printed in it. Now, Miss Pearle, tell us about William Faulkner.

P. Galloway: Okay.

F. Watkins: What kind of fellow was he?

P. Galloway: Did you know that in the late thirties and early forties when they first started the food program for the people who needed extra help and so on—they would just haul it out here and unload it in the store, and William Faulkner would give it to the people that needed it. Mr. William Faulkner was one of the ones that had something to do with that food program. Did you know that?[3]

J. Faulkner: No, I didn't.

P. Galloway: Well, he did. He might have been the big shot in it. I don't know what part he played, but he came out and got my daddy to handle the stuff, you know. Nobody signed up; they just came and got what they needed. It was mostly fruit and staple groceries. Being in business here, my father knew the ones that were not able to have what they needed. So he was the one that handed it out.

J. Faulkner: When they began restocking deer in this county in the 1930s in the restocking program, Brother Will set the first deer loose.

F. Watkins: Miss Pearle, your father owned this store?

P. Galloway: Yes.

F. Watkins: Did Faulkner ever come out and talk to him?

P. Galloway: Sure.

F. Watkins: I see. Did you see Faulkner often?

P. Galloway: Faulkner didn't come here often. He was here about the time my dad was living. I wasn't impressed with him. He wasn't sociable. My sister lived right close to him. She had a little girl that was about two years old that was a very friendly thing, and she would play out in the yard. Her yard was very, very small. The walk came almost right by their door. The little girl would just holler at everybody that came by. Everybody would holler at her, too, you know. So he would

3. The Surplus Commodities Program, established in 1933 and administered by the Federal Surplus Commodities Corporation, later became the Surplus Marketing Administration. Recipients of commodities included "families in low income groups whose resources [were] not sufficient to provide adequate subsistence." The school lunch program is first mentioned in the annual report of this group in 1939 as a relatively new program with plans to expand in the 1939–40 school year. The Mississippi State Department of Public Welfare mentions in its 1940–41 report that 865 schools participated in this program with 73,000 children served. The commodities distributed by the program made it possible for schools to furnish free lunches to underprivileged students (*Third Biennial Report, July 1, 1939–June 3, 1941* [Jackson, Mississippi, 1941], 32–33).

come by every day—he was walking, and she would holler "Hi!" He wouldn't say a word.

The next day, next time he passed here, it was the same thing. One day she went dashing inside, and she says, "Momma, Momma, Mr. Faulkner spoke to me!" She just thought that was the grandest thing he ever did. She finally did get him to speak. He just didn't pay any attention to anybody.

These people who hunted with him—and I had a very good friend who was one of the hunters—would tell all about all the hunting camp tales and everything. *Intruder in the Dust* was partly filmed in here. It was a school in the movie. It is still intact.[4]

J. Faulkner: You know there was a beauty shop operator here from out of the county. Some tourist asked her if she had read the works of John and William Faulkner. William Faulkner had already won the Nobel Prize. She said, "I don't read any of this local stuff."

F. Watkins: Miss Pearle, what do they call this vine?

P. Galloway: I really don't know. But it has a history. It was on the porch, the lattice porch over at our house that was built before the Civil War. The house burned, but for some reason it didn't quite kill the vine. My mother took it up and brought it over here.

F. Watkins: William Faulkner would know the name of this vine; he knew the name of every vine that ever grew.

P. Galloway: I bet he did, too. But, but I don't know what it is.

F. Watkins: Ever heard anybody call sardines "sourdines"?[5]

P. Galloway: No.

J. Faulkner: I have. It's a colloquialism down here.

F. Watkins: That's what he called them in *Light in August.*

P. Galloway: Oh, William Faulkner was just being different. He was very different.

---

4. Although Pearle Galloway's store was the setting for scenes in the film version of *Intruder in the Dust,* the store has no connection with the kind of store described in Faulkner's novel. The store is more typical of those that appear in other novels, such as *The Hamlet* and *The Mansion.*

5. *Cf.* Lena's colloquialism "sour-deens" in William Faulkner's *Light in August.*

Motee Daniel

Motee Daniel, a native of Oxford, in his seventies at the time of the interview, has lived a colorful life, owning various enterprises, including a general store and a road house (or juke joint). A natural humorist, politician, and raconteur, he tells stories to the delight of the groups of students and Faulknerians he considers "foreigners" who visit Oxford and the University of Mississippi. A great number of Faulkner's Yoknapatawpha characters resemble Motee Daniel.

Before meeting with Motee, Floyd Watkins and Jimmy Faulkner discuss his character and career, ranging from his fights, snakebites, and bouts with ring- and tapeworms to jokes about his entanglements with the government over the proper vaccination of his cattle. But Motee's own stories and jokes are even more hilarious than those told about him. Despite his modest protestations to the contrary, he can best any storyteller "two to one." Motee's lore about the curing of ailments and the characteristics of snakes shows him to be immersed in the rural culture Faulkner often depicted.

F. Watkins: Does Motee still live in his cabin?

J. Faulkner: Yes, he has a heck of a nice cabin out there—large. He bought the biggest, gaudiest, most lit-up record player you ever saw for his roadhouse. He's so proud of it. The lights come on and run across it like they did in old nickelodeons. Two years ago Motee said, "Let me let you listen to this thing." He played it for me.

F. Watkins: Well, Motee is funny. Is there a wild streak in Motee, or did he just watch the violence in other people?

J. Faulkner: There sure may be in him. I expect Motee has done about everything a man can in his day—at one time or another. He really made plenty of whiskey.

F. Watkins: Is he seeing us in his cabin?

J. Faulkner: Yes. It rained last night. We're going to Motee's the good way.

F. Watkins: If Motee gets started talking, he's funnier than anybody. He won't have anything to sell? Any white lightning?[6]

6. Homemade whiskey.

J. Faulkner: No, he stopped selling white lightning. He made enough to retire on.

F. Watkins: Did you tell me his store burned?

J. Faulkner: No, it closed. You heard about him getting his throat cut, didn't you?

F. Watkins: No.

J. Faulkner: Oh, it's the funniest thing you ever heard. His first wife left him because he worked her too much! Anyway, Tater Bowles and Motee were drinking alongside of the road; they pulled off to sit on the road bank. They had a jug, and they got into some kind of argument. The old fellow cut Motee's throat in a knife fight, cut it pretty damn bad. They got him to the hospital just in time and sewed him up, and it was nip and tuck whether he was going to live or not.

They put old Tater in jail; they felt bad about having to put him in jail, but they had to. When the fellow sobered up, he felt remorseful. He felt so bad about what he had done to Motee that he couldn't stand it; so he cut his own wrists trying to commit suicide. Well, they stopped him, took him down to the hospital, put him in the same room with Motee. It's a true story. They were good friends.

Anyway, a judge from up in Ripley was the judge for Motee's case. They had to try Tater, and they had to convict him, 'cause he said he cut his throat, but he didn't mean to. Just got all out of whack. Another time, a man was sentenced to six months in jail, but part of the sentence was that he would spend three weekends a month in jail, provided he'd go to church on Sundays. His wife would dress up in a long dress and sunbonnet and get him out of jail and take him to church. So he served his term that way.

F. Watkins: Last time I was here, Motee had his finger bit by a copperhead, and he had to go about with his finger pointed up that way. [Watkins holds up the index finger.]

J. Faulkner: So the blood would run back down to his feet.

F. Watkins: Well, I would like to get Motee to talk. Do you think Motee's going to have a steak dinner out here tonight?

J. Faulkner: Yes.

F. Watkins: Who'll come?

J. Faulkner: The Center for Southern Culture[7] will bring people from everywhere to see him.

F. Watkins: They'll be big shots; they won't be yokels. Has Motee got money?

J. Faulkner: Yes.

F. Watkins: He has? He doesn't do anything else to make money, or was bootlegging his primary source of income?

J. Faulkner: That's it. Later on he started to go legitimate a little bit. He was a salesman for Schenley's in Memphis, and Memphis was wet, so he could justify a little whiskey around.[8]

F. Watkins: Will you retell Motee's story about a cattle infection called Bang's disease?[9]

J. Faulkner: Inspectors test the cows that have this disease. They've had this big program going on here for the last ten years. The government men come around and test cows: if any of them tested have Bang's, you have to sell them. It doesn't affect the meat, but the government will pay you fifty dollars over what you get for a common herd cow or a hundred dollars over for a registered cow. But when you check them, and you have some in a herd tested with Bang's, then you say they've all banged out. You sell them. You can't cure them. When a cow has an infection or social disease like this, it can't carry a calf full term.

F. Watkins: The joke began when I asked Motee if he had any children.

J. Faulkner: Yes, that's right. He said, "No, Miss Lucille just banged out." Motee got real upset about the program. I was in the cattle association about the time Motee was involved. He said, "Do you

---

7. Center for the Study of Southern Culture at the University of Mississippi.

8. The Schenley Distillers Corporation consisted of thirty legalized distillers that produced whiskeys in Kentucky, Tennessee, and elsewhere. See Morris Victor Rosenbloom, *The Liquor Industry: A Survey of Its History, Manufacture, Problems of Control and Importance* (Braddock, Pa., 1936), 63–64; and *Moody's Industrial Manual* (New York, 1972), 2902–2903.

9. Bang's disease, *Bovine brucellosis,* is characterized by spontaneous abortion in late pregnancy and subsequent infertility in animals.

mean to tell me"—this was a big meeting here—"if I check my cows, and they check with Bang's, I've got to ship 'em to the slaughter house?" They said, "That's right," and he said, "What if my wife checks with Bang's? Have I got to get rid of her, too?" Cattle with Bang's can't have calves. So, when you asked about children, Motee told you Miss Lucille banged out!

F. Watkins: Tell us about the time you went with the Ole Miss tackle on the football team to Motee's juke joint in 1941.

J. Faulkner: Oh, I didn't know where they were going. This was back when I was a freshman at Ole Miss. Motee used to have his place out here in the community of Yocona, an old, one-room bootlegging and gambling place. And it was just about as tough as they come.

Now, a man who was a friend came by the house, and said, "Let's go out riding a bit," and I had a Model A Ford, and I said, "All right." So he and another friend got in and said, "Let's go out to Yocona." I said, "All right." So we got out here to Yocona. It was actually at Dutch Bend, which is between Tula and Toccopola. The night before, somebody had stolen a football player's wallet with his money in it. At the time I weighed right at one hundred and fifteen, and they weighed about two hundred or two-twenty apiece.

F. Watkins: They were big football players for that time.

J. Faulkner: Yes. We walked into that place, and it was full of people, country folks shooting craps, drinking. I just thought that I was going to have a look. But they all saw me come in with these two. The football player got a table, pulled it out in the middle of the floor, climbed up on top of it, and said, "Somebody stole my wallet last night, and I'm gonna whup every son of a bitch in here until I get it back." I said, "What have I got myself into?"

Anyway, someone threw the wallet out of a dark corner, and it landed on the table at his feet. He picked it up and counted, and it had his money in it. We left. That was Motee's place.

F. Watkins: Motee got another baby mule?

J. Faulkner: I told you he sold that mule, didn't I?

F. Watkins: No, I didn't know.

Fig. 43. Floyd Watkins (left) talking with Motee Daniel, after presenting him with a plaque from Emory University. Motee had recently moved to town. (*Courtesy of the Floyd C. Watkins Collection, Special Collections Department, Robert W. Woodruff Library, Emory University*)

J. Faulkner: Yes, he sold April. He named her that because she was born in April.

F. Watkins: Probably he could be a poet if he knew how to write.

J. Faulkner: Might ruin him if you tried to educate him too much.

F. Watkins: Yes. He didn't have an education, did he?

J. Faulkner: Not the kind you got in school.

F. Watkins: Well, I am sure glad his store didn't burn.

J. Faulkner: Think it was right along here someplace that he and that fellow were sitting around here drinking and got in that fight and the fellow cut his throat.

F. Watkins: How long ago was that, Jimmy?

J. Faulkner: About three or four years; not too long ago.

F. Watkins: Right about there, that's where he was bit by the copperhead?

J. Faulkner: On the index finger. Now, we're not too far from where we turn to the left, but it is a paved road. Motee's store is down toward the Yocona River.

Watch out for mules up here in the road. They're not Motee's.

F. Watkins: Those are donkeys, aren't they?

J. Faulkner: No.

F. Watkins: Mules that little?

J. Faulkner: Yes. Your big mules come from Missouri and Georgia, where you got a lot of lime in the soil.

F. Watkins: I never saw a mule that small in my life.

J. Faulkner: We got them around here. They're strong little devils, though.

F. Watkins: I would have bet you anything that wasn't a mule that small. Are they grown?

J. Faulkner: Yes. This is it; this is Motee's store. That's where the house next to it burned.

F. Watkins: I believe he's been in this morning, hasn't he?

J. Faulkner: Yes, he's been down there. He lives in that little, new, brick house back yonder by the store. This is just the cabin where he hangs out when there are tourists here. If I were you, I'd stop right at the door. He's got to be around here.

[Approaching Motee Daniel's juke joint. Eventually, Motee emerges from around the side of the building. He had been sitting around on the back step, as if he were waiting to visit with customers.]

F. Watkins: There he is. You got some drinks for us, haven't you?

M. Daniel: Let me see. I've got some Royal Crowns; yes, I got some Royal Crowns.[10]

F. Watkins: Motee, have you got much time?

M. Daniel: I sure haven't. No, I'm running bad late.

F. Watkins: Oh man, you got the place fixed up. Look at those paper towels nailed to that tree!

M. Daniel: Yes.

10. A once-popular cola drink.

F. Watkins: How is Lucille?

M. Daniel: Doing fine. You all didn't stop over there?

F. Watkins: Where is your copperhead bite?

M. Daniel: It's a little place right there—by this little *x*.

[Motee Daniel extends his index finger to reveal his scar from the bite of a copperhead.]

F. Watkins: Right, and all that purple streaked up your arm?

M. Daniel: No, that didn't bother me a bit, not a bit.

J. Faulkner: You know, I didn't know Miss Lucille is at her store. We're going back over there.

M. Daniel: That store is closed.

J. Faulkner: [Quail whistle.] We can get some drinks up that way at Ash's store.

F. Watkins: Can that fellow tell us as good stories while we buy drinks as you can, Motee?

M. Daniel: He can beat me two to one.

F. Watkins: Have you got five or ten minutes for us, or how much?

M. Daniel: Yes, sir, I'll take that much time with you. I'm really sorry that I got crowded this way, but this thing is running me to death the whole week, day and night. I got to prepare for sixty people of this Southern Cultural what?

J. Faulkner: Southern Cultural Center, yes.

M. Daniel: They are from all over the world: Europe, Egypt, and Switzerland. Bill Ferris[11] came by here to a party one night, and he didn't have no money, and I said, "It don't matter to me whether you got any or not." When he went back home, he wrote a check for five dollars and mailed it up here for the band.

J. Faulkner: Well, I'll be darn.

F. Watkins: Wrote a check for five dollars for a band?

M. Daniel: Well, we pass around the hat here. We don't pay no cover charge, you see. A bunch that comes in here tonight—the band will

11. William Ferris, director of the Center for the Study of Southern Culture at the University of Mississippi.

set up, and they'll pass around the hat. You know, like they used to; if you dance to the music, you've got to pay the fiddlers or they quit. When they quit, why you get the hat again.

F. Watkins: What did you do? Fiddle or hold the hat?

M. Daniel: No, I always get the best-looking girl in the house to pass the hat around.

F. Watkins: What did you do that for?

M. Daniel: Well, that's just more attraction. More than the boys. You know, they go around, and they'll just say, "Hell." They're going to keep this money in their pocket and buy a beer or buy their girlfriend a present. But they won't say that to the girls, you see.

F. Watkins: Well, was it you who was running the store that time when Jimmy came down with the two football players and somebody had lost his wallet?

M. Daniel: We still had the store then, I guess.

J. Faulkner: Yes, in Yocona when some fellows came out there; it was about 1940. One fellow said he was going to whip every man in the house until he got his wallet back.

M. Daniel: Well, I'll tell what he done; he like to kill a guy down at that house of mine. I guaran-damn-tee you, and that wasn't on account of a billfold. That was on account of getting this man's girlfriend.

F. Watkins: Can you tell the story?

M. Daniel: I thought he was going to kill him. He was stout. He was a big football player, right?

J. Faulkner: Oh, yes, he was.

M. Daniel: Man, he was tough.

F. Watkins: Can you tell me what happened to the girlfriend?

M. Daniel: Well, he was getting fresh with her, see; this man didn't like it, so they got in a fight about it, and I thought he was going to kill him. I swear I did.

F. Watkins: Well, you didn't get into it, did you, Motee?

M. Daniel: Oh, hell no, I've got more sense than that to get in it with one of those football players.

F. Watkins: You don't fight much yourself?

M. Daniel: My head feels like a sack of walnuts, and that's not the kind from the damn trees, now.

F. Watkins: Well, how'd you get them?

M. Daniel: Well, in them bars. If you ever run a juke house or a beer joint, you're going to have them.

F. Watkins: Did you enjoy them?

M. Daniel: Well, yes, I really did back then, but I couldn't do it today.

F. Watkins: You like to watch them?

M. Daniel: Oh, yes, you run my speedometer back about forty years, and I'd be back in there. But the chain broke.

F. Watkins: The speedometer chains broke?

M. Daniel: That's right. Well, you know it's like the old saying says that

> It's not the gray in your hair
> That makes you old,
> Or the wrinkles under your eyes,
> I've been told.
> But when your mind makes a date
> That your body can't take,
> Then you're old, you're old.

F. Watkins: Well, you're not in that shape, are you, Motee?

M. Daniel: Yes.

F. Watkins: You're just staying out of that shape, huh?

M. Daniel: That's right. Oh, I'm in good shape at my age. I guess we all are. But I see a whole lot of them that are in a whole lot worse shape than I am, that's younger than I am.

F. Watkins: Well, I might be a contender for that prize. Well, I certainly wouldn't try to catch copperheads. You still try to catch them with your feet?

M. Daniel: No. You know, I worked in Memphis up there with a fellow who was a snake man for the Overton Park Zoo. We rode together, rode every park in Memphis. I still thought it was a spreading adder;[12] you can't make a spreading adder bite you, and I had a stick just

---

12. A small, nonpoisonous southern snake, so called because of its cobralike hood.

behind his head there, and reached down. I didn't get that close to him, and don't think that they're not faster than your eye.

Now, I heard a story there in New Orleans, somewhere down in there, that they had one of them: they had this big rattlesnake down there, and this fellow was in there messing with the snake, and he had a balloon on the end of a cane. He got the snake real mad, and he told the people, "Now, don't watch the balloon, watch the snake. Now, don't take your eye off the snake." He was so fast; the balloon busted, and he never did see the snake move.

Now, I heard tell that they were down in one of those places where they show the reptiles, and all that stuff; you'll never see them. I didn't see them move, either. I don't know where I put the one that bit me, but I slung him somewhere, and I never did see him no more. He was hung to my finger, and, if a poisonous snake bites you, you don't have to go to the doctor to get him to tell you that the pain is right there, and you'll never have a pain like it.

F. Watkins: Bad, huh?

M. Daniel: Oh, God! But you know what, I fooled all the doctors. He just knew he was going to have to cut that finger off. It never did make me a bit sick, nothing in the world.

F. Watkins: Except that blue blood streak up your arm.

M. Daniel: Oh, yes, that's right.

F. Watkins: You had a big blue streak up your arm when I came that time, didn't you? After you'd got it bitten?

M. Daniel: It run a blue streak up there. [Motee points to his upper right arm.]

F. Watkins: And what did the doctor do?

M. Daniel: Well, he wrapped that thing up and said, "You want to live?" I said, "Who in the hell wants to die?" and he says, "Well, don't let that poison go below your heart. Hold it that-a-way" [Motee points upward]. So I carried my arm and finger around, and went to bed with it, and I'd wake up, and I'd grab it. I would never let it fall.

Well, I'll tell you right now. He give me a shot in the vein to counteract the poison, and I turned as red—as red as that towel there. Then I said, "God, you're burning me up." He jerked that out and shot another one in there. It counteracted that one. I said, "All right," and he says, "You don't feel sick?" I said, "I ain't a bit sick," and he says, "I can't believe that." It never did make me the least bit sick. But you talk about pain!

F. Watkins: How long did you have to carry your finger that way, Motee?

M. Daniel: Well, about a week. I slept with it that way. You had to sleep with it and get a pillow and prop it up, and you'd feel like it was getting you. Grab that thing; don't let it go down!

F. Watkins: Well, you still got your mule?

M. Daniel: No, I sold that mule.

F. Watkins: Well, now, did you keep the baby mule?

M. Daniel: No, that's the one we sold.

F. Watkins: Oh, I see. But you owned a mule, the mare that had the mule, didn't you?

M. Daniel: No, I sold her.

F. Watkins: You sold her, too? What was the mule's name?

M. Daniel: April. That mule is—ain't no telling how many thousands of dollars worth of pictures have been made of that mule, is it? Pictures—films and stuff—been took of that mule.

F. Watkins: You mean city people like these kids coming around?

M. Daniel: She's been in the *Mid South Magazine* of the *Commercial Appeal.*

F. Watkins: Is that right? Well, why was this such an unusual mule?

M. Daniel: Well, there's just no mules in this country hardly any more, and she was just a pet; I raised her, and she was just a pet.

F. Watkins: What was her mama's name?

M. Daniel: I don't know if she was a registered Tennessee Walker.[13] I don't even know. They just called her Dolly, that's all.

F. Watkins: Dolly.

---

13. Also called a plantation walking horse. A breed of horse deriving its name from the state of Tennessee and for its running walk, a trait bred to ensure comfort for the rider and to cover great distances at considerable speed.

M. Daniel: But I had the papers on her. She was a Tennessee Walker, all right. But she had three gaits; start, stumble, and fall! She didn't have a gait you could set on. It was like beating you on the back with a mall. She just didn't have it. First time I ever saw a registered horse that wasn't gaited.

F. Watkins: How old was she when you bought her, Motee?

M. Daniel: She was about eight, I think. I got her from a feller up here at New Albany, and I sold that mule to a chap down here that sells the furniture. I said, "Do you want this mule? Are you going to keep her?" He said, "Oh, hell, I wouldn't get rid of her for nothing. I got a mare down there that wants to keep her company." That chap has got a lot of money. [Quail whistle.] I said, "Well, all right. She'll have a good home; that's all right."

Well, you know what he done with her. That mule trader down in Paris, you know. He tried to sell her to him for five hundred. He wouldn't take her, so he hired Billy to carry her to New Albany, and he lost forty dollars on her. She brought a hundred and sixty, and he lost that.

F. Watkins: But horse trading used to be a lot of fun in this country, didn't it?

M. Daniel: Oh, yes, there was many a horse man. You know, I was telling you one time about the way you worm horses. There wasn't no such thing as worm medicine to worm a horse. But homemade chewing tobacco—you grew it. My daddy—they didn't buy no tobacco. They grew it and put it in sweetened water if they wanted sweet tobacco and get it good and damp and roll it up and chew it. We'd tell them about it, and whenever you wanted to worm the horses, you'd chop up some of that in their feed. Didn't a one of the students believe it, but that's what they used that tobacco for. They looked at me like I was crazy.

F. Watkins: Well, now, they used to worm—what did they used to worm children with?

M. Daniel: Walpool's Worm Oil. God!

F. Watkins: How do you spell "Walpool"?

M. Daniel: I don't know, but that's what it was.

F. Watkins: What was so bad about it, the way—

M. Daniel: [Moans.] Oh, God!

F. Watkins: The way it tasted?

M. Daniel: Now, I don't know why.

F. Watkins: Or how it made you feel?

M. Daniel: I don't know why, nobody would believe it. Jimmy knows it, and people our age know it. But people don't have worms today; I don't ever hear of it. Back then, my God, you'd have—well—you won't believe it, but they would crawl out of you at night. [Interviewers moan.] If there's a God in heaven, I never told the truth in my life if that ain't the truth. What in hell caused them, God only knows.

J. Faulkner: You get them by eating wormy food. There was no refrigeration back then. Meat was smoked, but flies would get in it. Milk was kept in the spring or the well house. That was the coolest place they could find. There were lots of opportunities to get worms.

F. Watkins: But Walpool would get rid of them.

M. Daniel: There wasn't anything back then but that. I don't know whether it was the food we was eating or what it was. Everybody had them then, didn't they?

J. Faulkner: I think so.

F. Watkins: What kind of worms were they, Motee?

M. Daniel: They were just a big, old, long worm, I don't know. It wasn't a tapeworm—people had tapeworms.

F. Watkins: Well, what's the difference?

M. Daniel: Well, it's spread out and looks like a tape. But these are round ones.

F. Watkins: By the way, have you ever heard of a hoop snake and joint snakes?[14]

14. The glass snake, known for its smooth, glassy skin, is sometimes referred to as the joint or brittle snake. In lore it is thought to be brittle, so that the slightest touch will break it into pieces, but, uniquely, this snake can pull itself back together. See Raymond Lee Ditmars, *The Reptiles of North America: A Review of the Crocodilians, Lizards, Snakes, Turtles and Tortoise Inhabiting the United States and Northern Mexico* (New York, 1936), 82–84. The hoop snake can allegedly take its tail in its mouth and roll like the rim of a wagon wheel. Ditmars thinks that this is a folk belief deriving from the "circular posture sometimes assumed by the snake when resting in inundated grass," so that it resembles a bicycle tire. The coachwhip snake is said to have a tail like a leather whip with which it whips or even wraps around and kills its victim. The blue racer, common in the lower Mississippi valley, is bluish green in color.

M. Daniel: Oh, yeah.

F. Watkins: Are there such things?

M. Daniel: There's a snake—you hit it, and it will fall all to pieces. They're medieval. But the book says that it's a lizard.

F. Watkins: Oh, it does?

M. Daniel: Yeah, a reptile book.

F. Watkins: You read about those in a book?

M. Daniel: Oh, I've killed them.

F. Watkins: You have?

M. Daniel: Killed many a one, yes. Every country boy in the county calls them glass snakes. Oh, yes.

F. Watkins: We call them joint snakes. Did you ever see them split apart, and you saw them go back together?

M. Daniel: I never did see them go back together, but I never figured that I had enough time. But I've hit them, and they'll just break up all to pieces.

Now, I've never seen your hoop snake, and I've seen your coachwhip snake. Now, that's the prettiest snake I've ever saw in my life. They'll grow to be about—well, I hung one up over here at the store that somebody ran over. I saw one the other day, I bet a hundred dollars, back yonder side of the feed mill run across the road, and I've never saw such a long snake, and them things can slide. But that was a long one. This one was killed down here on the other side of Yocona. But from about that long, at the end of their tail, looks just exactly like a whip. You ever see one of those things?

J. Faulkner: Yes.

M. Daniel: They're beautiful.

F. Watkins: That's why they call them a coachwhip?

M. Daniel: Coachwhip.

F. Watkins: That's not the same thing as a racer.

M. Daniel: No, no—blue racer?

J. Faulkner: No, a blue racer don't look too long, but, boy, can it fly.

M. Daniel: But it can fly, get its head up, and yonder it goes. That's right.

F. Watkins: Well, I believe that we have taken as much time as we should. We didn't get here earlier because there are so many other interesting things to see.

M. Daniel: Yes, well, like I say, I wish that I could spend the evening with you and get out of this work.

F. Watkins: Well, we don't want to keep you too long. You don't figure on opening up your store again?

M. Daniel: I never did; that's Lucille's. I don't know what she's going to do. Don't nobody know what that woman's going to do but her. That's the only person in the world that I've ever seen that wasn't flexible. I could always bend somebody, but I've never moved her one-tenth of a thousand. Now, that's her. She runs her show, and I run mine.

F. Watkins: It's always been that way?

M. Daniel: Ever since we've been married. She can't move me and I can't—

F. Watkins: Who ran the show before you were married, Motee?

M. Daniel: Well, I did. But the thing changed when I said, "I do." Do you agree with me?

F. Watkins: Well, do you remember I asked you one time if you had some children, you remember how you said it?

M. Daniel: I don't remember.

F. Watkins: You said, "No, Miss Lucille is banged out."

M. Daniel: Yes, I believe that's what I said.

J. Faulkner: She didn't change the expression on her face, either.

F. Watkins: Tell us what "banged out" is.

M. Daniel: I used to have all this cattle over here. Whenever I was still in the cabin out there, and here come all them guys to test the cattle. I sold some; they found the bangin' in them, and then they get your whole herd. Talk about hell, that's hell. You've got to run them down, whenever you stick them two or three times; God, they get so wild. They'll run you out of the pen and all that stuff, and you can't get them up.

Well, I was building this cabin, me and another boy down here. We built that with a handsaw and a hammer; there wasn't no electricity on that there. I cut them logs and had them sawed, sawed at the mill, and we nailed that up, every bit of it. Sawed it all with a handsaw and built it. They come down here; they done arrested me twice up there. You remember, I got up and made a big talk down about the McCarthyism?

F. Watkins: What did they arrest you for, Motee?

M. Daniel: 'Cause I brought back some cattle that was banged up there, and they all had calves beside 'em, and I told them, "I thought you all wanted cattle that would raise calves." Now, they're stealing them, wasn't they? I said, "You steal our cows; we go to the butcher shop; we pay just as much for that banged piece of meat as you do that for any other kind. Why in the hell don't you put a *B* on it so we'll know that it's banged? We'll know it will be cheaper that way." They vaccinate them so they can't reproduce—that's supposed to get rid of them Bang's. They raise calves, but the ones that I had, that were vaccinated, they're all banged out, and they had calves beside them. And so I got up there, and I told them, you know. Hell, I stood up quick.

J. Faulkner: Yes, I know.

M. Daniel: Yes, I told them. I told two or three of the supervisors, and they said, "What in the hell's wrong with you?" I said, "I'm mad!" Anybody'd be mad whenever they take your cattle like that, you know.

J. Faulkner: Yes.

M. Daniel: But now on the registered stuff they'll pay you, what, a hundred dollars?

J. Faulkner: A hundred dollars, I think.

M. Daniel: That helps. But they wanted me to quit building this cabin and help run these cattle up, and I said, "You got them so wild now, I don't know where you'd ever catch them." I said, "Tell me what causes the Bang's, and maybe we can settle this right here, for I ain't going to stop driving nails. You all can arrest me or send me to Parchman[15] or do whatever you want to." I said, "Tell me, Doc, what causes it?" Some guy from Jackson was up here. He said, "Well, a doe deer, a fox, and a female dog—they get it some way or another, I don't know." Then they figure some way that's the way you catch them.

15. The Mississippi State Penitentiary, a prison farm. In Faulkner's novel *The Town,* Mink Snopes spends thirty-eight years of his life there.

I said, "I'll tell you what I'll do, and you won't have to mess with me anymore. If you'll keep all the female dogs and foxes, go out there and open the gap, you can have every damn one of them. I'm through with it." I said, "I ain't going to run the cows no more." They'd slip around and watch. I told them I sold them. You know, I lied to them; I done everything I could. I told them I sold them, and ol' Jim would come up and see them somewhere and report it to them. We had a lot of fun out of it.

[Outside Motee's juke joint.]

F. Watkins: Well, Motee, we're keeping you. It sure has been fun. Next time when we come, we'll let you know ahead of time, and we'll just eat supper with you.

M. Daniel: I wish you would, if you do, we'll have a party; we'll have a party over here. My lodge is north two or three miles from here by a lake. That's where the jukebox is and where I can have these parties.

F. Watkins: Will you give it to us at the same rate that you're giving this one tonight?

M. Daniel: I sure as hell will. It ain't costing me a penny. They're paying me. I guarantee that. I'll tell you something. There's $152.79 for the steaks, and that's $18.00 for the baked potatoes, plus that's about $300.00 more than that, for drinks and stuff like that.

F. Watkins: I see, and who are these people coming? The whole world, you say?

M. Daniel: Yes, yes.

F. Watkins: Well, it's been mighty nice of you.

M. Daniel: It's been a pleasure. If you'll let me know the next time about a week ahead of time, something like that, we'll have a ball.

F. Watkins: If you hear some real good stories, write them and tell me about them, Motee.

M. Daniel: I sure will.

F. Watkins: Did you know William Faulkner?

M. Daniel: Well, who didn't know William, our age? Well, let me see how are you all going to get out of here.

J. Faulkner: You reckon we can get through this gate here?

M. Daniel: Yes, just tie it back. Hang that nail on the post, and whenever you open it with that thing, that nail on the top of the post will shut.

[Departing Motee's.]

F. Watkins: Now, there's an old house. What kind is that? That's a log house.

J. Faulkner: Doesn't look too good.

F. Watkins: Did you say that Motee's in his seventies?

J. Faulkner: Well, he was running a road house when I was seventeen years old, back in the late thirties.

F. Watkins: I think his best joke was the Tennessee walking horse that had three gaits: start, stumble, and fall.

J. Faulkner: Start, stumble, and fall.

F. Watkins: Have you ever heard that one before?

J. Faulkner: No. He tried to talk me into breeding all my mares to a jack one time. I would have had all mules out there.

F. Watkins: What is it they call it when they breed a female horse to a jack?

J. Faulkner: That's a mule.

F. Watkins: Right. What's the other?

J. Faulkner: The other is a henny. Breed a jenny, a female donkey, to a stallion and you get a henny.

F. Watkins: Can you tell the difference by looking between them?

J. Faulkner: I believe that the only difference is that a henny ain't got any sense; you can't do anything with it.

5

A NEPHEW REMEMBERS WILLIAM FAULKNER

In fact, the ground itself never let a man forget it was there waiting, pulling gently and without no hurry at him between every step, saying, come on, lay down; I aint going to hurt you. Jest lay down.

— *The Mansion*

Jimmy Faulkner recollects his uncle and his family from both the biased view of an appreciative nephew and the more objective view of a man who knew Faulkner well as family man, hunting buddy, and friend. He recounts stories about life at Rowan Oak with William and Estelle. He remembers, for example, taking baths out of the cistern; Faulkner's drinking habits; the trip William and Estelle made to a whorehouse in Memphis; his complete trust of his uncle: "I believed everything that he said"; and, in words similar to Faulkner's self-definition: "He said he was not a historian but rather a recorder. He wrote what he saw and heard." He remembers his uncle's last days, Faulkner's last words to him, trouble with the casket, and the family and community's reaction to each other at the time of the death.

S. Wolff: Did you have a good time with your uncle when you were growing up?

J. Faulkner: Oh, yes He had the ability to operate on anybody's level. He got down on the floor with me when I was two and played with me, often. He was crazy about children. When I was young, we all used to live together at the university because Big Dad was secretary and treasurer of Ole Miss, and my daddy went to engineering school there. Brother Will was living there because he wasn't making enough money to live anywhere else. He and Dean lived on the east side on the sleeping porch; we lived on the other side of the hall. I stayed in Brother Will and Dean's room and played with them. I used to play in Brother Will's room, and I had more fun playing with him than with my mother and daddy. He taught me to call him Brother Will when I got old enough to talk.

S. Wolff: Would you say more about William Faulkner as a family man?

J. Faulkner: Well, he worshiped Nanny, his mother. She had such an overpowering personality that just her desire was a command, and there was never any uproar. People worshiped her, really. Especially her boys. [Laughter.] Dean and Louise[1] were married in, I think, 1933. But the minute they were married, Dean turned to Louise and said, "You know, mother comes first." [Laughter.] That's the way to start a marriage.

S. Wolff: At what age did William Faulkner know he was going to be a writer?

J. Faulkner: When Brother Will was six, he said, "I'm going to write books like Great-Granddaddy did."

F. Watkins: Did William Faulkner's father enjoy his son's success as a writer?

J. Faulkner: No. See, Big Dad didn't live long enough; Big Dad died in '32. Brother Will was just coming into his writing then. He wanted Brother Will to write cowboy stories. He hit the ceiling when Brother Will wrote *Sanctuary.* Once he took the book away from an Ole Miss coed and said, "This book is not fit for you to read." Big Dad

---

1. Louise Hale.

talked to Nanny about it. Nanny said, "Buddy, leave him alone. He writes what he has to." Big Dad did. Of course, Big Dad was always mad at Nanny because she wouldn't move out west so he could be a cowboy.

Someone once asked Brother Will why he wrote *Sanctuary*. Brother Will said he thought of the worst thing that could happen to a woman and wrote it to sell. He said he hoped nobody lends it to anyone else to read. Make them buy it. He wrote it for the money.[2]

F. Watkins: Was the William Faulkner marriage made out of love as it might have been?

J. Faulkner: I don't know. It's like trying to tell someone what goes on in somebody else's house. I remember that Brother Will would come get me to come and play with Malcolm while he courted Aunt Estelle.

S. Wolff: Would you describe Faulkner's relationship with his daughter?

J. Faulkner: It was real good. He thought the sun rose and set on her.

F. Watkins: What was William Faulkner like to you, not as a writer, not as an uncle, but as a man?

J. Faulkner: No way in hell to answer that question. We had a real good, buddy-buddy relationship.

S. Wolff: Did you continue to stay with William Faulkner after he was married?

J. Faulkner: I lived with him a couple of years in the same house when he was still living at home. After he and Aunt Estelle married, I spent the night with them often—this was before there were lights and water—and I stayed with them at Rowan Oak, too. He, Malcolm, and I would go out to the cistern and draw up water and pour it over each other to take baths. We slept on pallets out on the hall floor. This continued for three years after he and Aunt Estelle had been married.

I played with Malcolm often. We had blank pistols and rubber guns. Brother Will didn't like to drive much, so from the time I was fifteen, he would call me and ask if I'd drive him to Memphis for the day.

2. See *Faulkner at Nagano*, ed. Robert A. Jelliffe (Tokyo, 1956), 9, 63–64.

He gave me directions once. I was going to Cherry Point, North Carolina, one time. I was in the Marine Corps then. Brother Will was being real helpful. He said, "I'm going to show you how to get to Atlanta so you won't have to go through Birmingham." He did. He directed me onto gravel roads, and it took me about five hours longer to get there than ordinarily. He said that's the way he went. When I got back, I said, "You can go that way all you want to; I'm never going to do that again." By ten o'clock that night, I finally got to Atlanta. I was miserable. He thought he knew a short cut, but it was really longer.

F. Watkins: Was William your favorite uncle?

J. Faulkner: I ain't going to tell you who my favorite uncle was. They were entirely different people. I guess I admired Jack as a real man more than anybody else.

S. Wolff: Did William and his brother John talk often?

J. Faulkner: John and Brother Will talked all the time. No one knew I could talk till I was thirty-nine years old. After both Brother Will and John died, I said something one day, and everyone turned around and listened. I thought to myself, "Well, I'll be damned."

S. Wolff: Are there any particular stories that you've heard or seen written after your uncle's death that you especially find to be untrue?

J. Faulkner: Nothing that he didn't perpetuate himself! Brother Will was compassionate; the hard side of him was a veneer. He did not like people to get close to him, because they could hurt him. That's one reason he stayed away from people. He did not believe in suicide like Quentin [Compson]. When Mr. Hemingway died, that shook him pretty hard, and he said, "He took the easy way out." He didn't believe in suicide.[3]

S. Wolff: Were there any suicides in your family?

J. Faulkner: No. No, we never had anybody commit suicide. Not on purpose. We had some family members do some damn foolish things—one even got shot and killed—but they didn't do it on purpose.

S. Wolff: Why did William Faulkner like to say he was uneducated?

3. See Blotner, *Faulkner: A Biography,* II, 1790, for further details on Faulkner's reaction to Hemingway's suicide.

J. Faulkner: Brother Will liked to say that because he didn't have his diploma from anywhere. Brother Will didn't lie, but he stretched the hell out of the truth at times. That was the truth; he didn't have a diploma of any sort.

Nanny directed her children's reading from the time they were big enough to open up a book, and all four boys skipped some grades from grammar school to high school because they had read Conrad, Shakespeare, the Bible, and a number of the real books, you know. So he was really a self-educated man.

He got to go to college as a special student on fifteen credits from high school, where it takes sixteen credits to get a diploma. The other credit might be basketball, football, or something like that. So he went as a special student, and his first semester he took Spanish, French, and English. He made an A in Spanish, a B in French, a D in English, and he dropped English. He tried one more semester, I think, and then he quit school.[4]

John, my daddy, did teach creative writing at Ole Miss one year. I don't know how many were in the class—I'd say ten or fifteen—but he told them, "Your final grade is going to be based on a short story or a novelette that you write this semester." He said, "We'll help all of you all through the year, all through the semester."

There was one boy who couldn't get his story together in time—he played baseball. So he went to the drug store. It had a book rack of paperback novels—they used to sell for a quarter, thirty-five cents, something like that. The student went down, and he found the thinnest little book he could find way back in the corner, in an insignificant place; bought it; copied it; and turned it in. John said, "I'll be in the office on such and such an afternoon, and you can get your final grade."

The students were lined up outside on that day, going in, coming out with their grades, and this one boy just knew that he had an A because he had copied somebody who had been published. He went in all

4. According to Blotner, Faulkner enrolled in the fall of 1919 and received an A in French, a B in Spanish, and a D in English, which he dropped. He withdrew from the university on November 5, 1920 (*ibid.*, I, 250, 287).

smiling and came out with his mouth open four inches wide, and somebody asked him, "What did you get?" He said, "I got an *F*." And he said, "Well, what'd he say?" John had said to him, "I didn't like it the first time I read it." [Laughter.]

S. Wolff: How do you view your uncle's opinion of racial prejudice?

J. Faulkner: He was a seer, prophet, whatever you want to call it. He had the ability to see what was going to happen in the future. In a letter to the editor, he once wrote that the federal government should let us in the South settle our own problems: don't try to force us—it will not work. I don't know whether I'm answering your question, but that's the way he felt.

S. Wolff: What is your opinion about the portrayal of the black characters in at least several of Faulkner's works who have the deepest resources of moral fortitude, such as Dilsey and Lucas Beauchamp?

J. Faulkner: Most of the people he writes about were modeled after individuals he knew and who had been close to the family a long time, like James, Mammy Callie, and Uncle Ned. But, then, some characters are ambiguous—Joe Christmas wasn't even sure what he was. He wasn't sure. That was his problem. But Brother Will did not believe in using force.

S. Wolff: To integrate?

J. Faulkner: To integrate or to change society. You can't legislate society.

Let me tell you how he felt about Hollywood. He hated it; he didn't like it at all. He said Hollywood is too superficial; he said he was a Mississippian.

Two or three days after Nanny died, Jack was here and was sitting on a curb in front of Nanny's house, and Jack was getting ready to go back to Mobile. I asked Brother Will if he was going to live in Virginia, now that Nanny was gone, and he said, "No, I'll never change my lifestyle; I'm a Mississippian." He didn't like California. He said he didn't know any literary people.

S. Wolff: Did William Faulkner write according to a time schedule?

J. Faulkner: Yes, Brother Will had a writing schedule. He would work half a day or four or five hours and take the rest of the day off to let his mind unwind. He was an outdoor type of person. I would imagine his work was on his mind a lot, like anybody else's occupation would be, but he didn't sit down to think, Now, that's what I'm going to do tomorrow. He was just a normal person.

S. Wolff: He revised a lot, didn't he?

J. Faulkner: Oh, yes, he was never satisfied. Even when he finished a story, he wasn't satisfied with it, but that was the perfectionist in him. If he didn't know how to spell a word or something, he would hunt until he found it. He called me once to ask about what they call brand-new second lieutenants in the service.

S. Wolff: He said he wasn't satisfied with, among others, *The Sound and the Fury,* the book that he said "failed four times."[5]

J. Faulkner: That's right. He was a perfectionist.

Do you know about his post office experience?[6] He was investigated by the postmaster general. He didn't want the job to begin with, and Phil Stone maneuvered him into it. He was the post office. He was the only employee. He was the postmaster, the janitor, what have you, and everything in between. All the mail that came in had to go out the window. There were no deliveries and no post office boxes.

He used to sit behind the window, so he could hand out the mail through it, like at a bank teller's window, and the table he sat at was about the size of a card table. He would read as people came to get their mail, and, if he didn't like them, he wouldn't give them their mail. He wouldn't even look up, and he didn't like very many people, either.

He had most of the mail left at the end of the day, and he liked to have a clean desk at night. So he would take the mail and dump it in the garbage can in the back. The professors had to go out and scratch through garbage every day to get their mail, and they thought that was beneath their dignity. So they got in touch with the postmaster general in Wash-

5. See Jelliffe, ed., *Faulkner at Nagano,* 103–105.
6. See Faulkner, *my brother Bill,* 142–43, for corroboration of the story.

ington to have Brother Will investigated. He quit and said, "I'm not going to be at the beck and call of every son of a bitch who has two cents to swap for a stamp. Besides, I didn't like the job anyway."[7] I'll bet he laughed when a postage stamp was dedicated to him with his picture on it because people would have to lick his back to glue the stamp to a letter. [Laughter.]

S. Wolff: Why do you think your family has been so interested in horsemanship?

J. Faulkner: Uncle Ned once told me that the Old Colonel had a horse named Pompous. Uncle Ned said he could tell when the Old Colonel was coming home because he could hear Pompous' hoofbeats on the wooden bridge up to the farm he had in Ripley.

I do have a funny story about a dog! Brother Will did have this reputation for not opening mail. But once he opened a letter from a lady from out of town. She had a new dog and asked him what to name it. So he wrote "Fido" on the card and walked to town, laughing, and mailed it.

S. Wolff: What were your uncle's other leisure activities besides hunting and fishing?

J. Faulkner: He played tennis. Back in about the early to mid-1930s, Bob and Sally Williams had a dirt tennis court in their back yard. We would go down and play tennis anytime we could.

One afternoon, John (my daddy) and I were playing as a team against Brother Will and somebody else—I can't remember who. At that time I was about ten or maybe twelve years old, and I was doing a good bit of playing on our team. John was letting me. Brother Will lobbed a tennis ball a little over my head, but it was good—in the court. I returned it as a good ball. I was at the back side of the court, and the ball landed right in front of Brother Will, and he barely tipped it over the net. Well, I ran as hard as I could, but I could not get close to the ball. John said, "Bill, that was a dirty thing to do." Brother Will said, "Well, he's got to learn."

S. Wolff: Did you play tennis with them often?

J. Faulkner: Well, a good bit because he made a dirt tennis court down behind where his stable is now at Rowan Oak. We played tennis

---

7. See Blotner, *Faulkner, A Biography,* I, 365, for confirmation.

down there or anyplace else we had a chance because that was the one sport just a few people could play, and we didn't have that many people in Oxford who could actually play.

S. Wolff: Was he a good player?

J. Faulkner: Pretty good.

S. Wolff: Besides you, did he play with anyone else?

J. Faulkner: Any of the boys who wanted to play. He played with mainly our age because he liked to be with us rather than people his age.

S. Wolff: Who taught him to play?

J. Faulkner: I guess he just picked it up, as far as I know. A lot of people had dirt tennis courts back then. When we lived on the Ole Miss campus out there when Big Dad worked there, he was furnished a house. Brother Will and Dean lived with him. We would sit on the front gallery and watch out in the front yard because there was a dirt tennis court out there. A lot of students came over to play, and sometimes he would play with them. As far as I can remember back, he played tennis.

S. Wolff: Did he play other games like tennis?

J. Faulkner: He loved croquet, and he liked to swim. He played football in high school: that is how he broke his nose. You know how it's mashed out of shape a little bit? He got it tackling one of our own men. Brother Will was a quarterback. The team had an end named Possum McDaniels. Possum couldn't catch a football. When he would go down for a pass, the other team wouldn't even cover him.

One day we were playing Holly Springs, our rival up north about thirty miles from Oxford, and the score was tied, or real close. Brother Will said, "Possum, they don't expect me to throw a football to you; I'm going to throw it to you, and you are going to catch it." So Possum went running down the field, and Brother Will threw it to him, and he caught it! Possum was so excited he got mixed up and started running the wrong way. Brother Will tackled him to keep him from going over the wrong goal line, and that's how he broke his nose.[8] Possum McDaniels died two or three years ago. He became one of the top surgeons in Muleshoe, Texas.

8. See *ibid.,* 166, for further details.

S. Wolff: Did he ever read his works aloud?

J. Faulkner: He did like to read to people. There were times in the afternoon he would read to Aunt Estelle. When he was through with a chapter or some passage, he would read to her. But this was early, early in the game. Later on he didn't. One time, Aston Holley—Aston is my age, but this was when he was about twelve, I guess. We were playing with Malcolm, Brother Will's stepson; we were about the same age—and there were three or four of us playing down at Rowan Oak that afternoon. Well, Malcolm and I were there earlier, and we were playing down on the back side of the house—the west side.

Brother Will was sitting in a chair in the east-side yard proofreading some of his work, and Aston ran by and said, "Hi, Mr. Bill, what are you doing?" Brother Will said, "I'm reading some of this. Would you like to hear it?" Aston wanted to come around to where we were playing, but he was real nice, and he said, "Yes, sir." Aston was barefooted and had short pants on, and Brother Will knew what he was doing. Brother Will started reading to him, and he read a long time. Aston was standing on one foot and then the other, and all he wanted to do was get back and play with us. Finally, after he had read about five or six pages to Aston, Brother Will said, "Aston, what did you think about that?" Aston said, "Just fine, Mr. Bill, just fine,"[9] and he turned around and left. Brother Will had read him a part of *The Sound and The Fury*. Yes, he read to some people!

S. Wolff: Would you comment upon the effect of storytelling around Oxford upon your uncle?

J. Faulkner: Oh, yes. A long time ago, with no radio and television, the entertainment at night was sitting around the fireplace, and many times there were three or sometimes four generations living in the same house. So the older generation would tell stories and legends that had come down through the family or different things that had happened, that they heard around town, around the country. When I read some of Brother Will's stories the first time, I thought, "Hell, I know this

9. *Cf.* Marshall, "Scenes from Yoknapatawpha," 306.

story." He fictionalized many stories and used them as a base for an expanded story. Almost everything he wrote had a base.

S. Wolff: In the old tales?

J. Faulkner: Yes.

S. Wolff: What was the community's reaction to Faulkner's work?

J. Faulkner: Well, after *The Sound and The Fury* came out, Arthur MacIntosh—an Oxford lawyer—his daddy filled two pages full of commas and periods and sent it to Brother Will and said, "This is what you left out."

S. Wolff: Your uncle liked to help the members of the community, though, didn't he? I'm thinking, in particular, of your story about the ditch that William Faulkner dug out on his farm to help drain his neighbor's farm so they could make a crop.

J. Faulkner: Puskus Creek. When he sold *Intruder in the Dust* and made it to the movies, he used some of the money to channel Puskus Creek. The channeling helped drain the land for his neighbors so they could make a crop each year. It stopped the flooding of Puskus Creek when it was raining too much to plant. It saved his neighbor's farm.

F. Watkins: Tell us about what William Faulkner said about spending money.

J. Faulkner: Oh, it started off with the bird dog. We kept bird dogs together, and about a week before bird season opened one year, our bird dog died. It was a tradition for us to hunt on the opening day of quail season. I went down to see Brother Will and said, "Look, our dog's dead, and bird season opens next week." He said, "You come down here on opening day."

So I got down there, and he had one of the prettiest pair of dogs I ever saw. They hunted like champions. I asked him where he got the dogs, and he told me. I said, "What'd you pay for them?" He said, "Five hundred dollars." I said, "Great day! I could have gotten ten dogs like that for that amount of money." He said, "Let me tell you something. Any time you can swap money for pleasure, do it."[10] [Laughter.]

10. See Blotner, *Faulkner: A Biography,* II, 1810, and Marshall, "Scenes from Yoknapatawpha," 263.

A couple of his feist dogs were named Flicker and Adeline.

S. Wolff: Why do you think William Faulkner had such distinct styles of dress?

J. Faulkner: Brother Will lived the way he wanted to. His clothes—when he had to go some place for the State Department—the clothes he had to wear, the formals he had to rent—he didn't care a damn thing about clothes. But his hunting clothes came from England, and his riding clothes were the best. The dress-up clothes were elegant, but he looked like a sharecropper most of the time.

S. Wolff: What else do you recall him saying that impressed you?

J. Faulkner: He had clever sayings. One time we were in traffic in Memphis, and he said, "One day a car will come off the assembly line and take the last slot, and our whole transportation system is going to be gridlocked." Another time a man came up to Brother Will and asked if he would endorse his product called Red Rooster Snuff. Brother Will said, "I knew there was something missing in my life, but I didn't know it was Red Rooster Snuff."

S. Wolff: Do you know any other hunting stories about your uncle?

J. Faulkner: You know Brother Will's story, "A Bear Hunt"? You know that boy who had the hiccups? Brother Will was the one who had the hiccups. Dan Ferguson was the pharmacist in Batesville, Mississippi. He went to get something for the hiccups. He was at the hunting camp when it happened. The pharmacist opened the drug store that night to get him something for it.

S. Wolff: What did the pharmacist give him to cure the hiccups?

J. Faulkner: Probably a drink! Sometimes I get the hiccups, and it lasts twenty-four hours. But Brother Will did not drink nearly as much as people said he did. He drank a lot, but in spurts. He had a set time to get drunk and a set time to sober up. In between there was nothing but alcohol. [Laughter.] Brother Will was anything but a hypocrite about his drinking. He would just as soon drink on the square, and, if anyone didn't want to, that person could go home. Once, William and John both got drunk at the same time. John was active all the time. Brother Will was active the first day, then he went to bed.

They had a party here when they got through filming *Intruder in the Dust*. Nanny wanted to go up and watch it, so he took her up there. Brother Will had been on the reservoir sailing that afternoon. He came in just a sweatshirt, old, dirty duck pants, probably tennis shoes or something like that, and needed a shave. Somehow, Nanny was there—I guess Sallie Murry Wilkins took her—I don't know, but anyway, Brother Will went like that, and everyone else was dressed up. So Nanny made him go home, clean up, and put some decent clothes on. He came back, and they tried to give him a cocktail, and he said, "No." They said, "Don't you want to toast the finishing of the film?" He said, "No, I want to get drunk a week from Tuesday. I'm not going to drink until then." He wouldn't. He could get sort of cantankerous when he wanted to be. When people pushed him, that's when he became rebellious.

He had a wreck once in Chattanooga. He told me about it, and then he got embarrassed; I don't think he told anybody else about it. He had that little red Nash station wagon until he died. Jill and Paul[11] took it back to Virginia with them, and I was talking to Jill one time, and she said, "That thing drives funny." I said, "You know, it's been wrecked, don't you?" She said, "No!"

He and Aunt Estelle were coming back from Virginia, and in Chattanooga they had a wreck. Not a bad one, but it bent the frame a little, and the man he had a wreck with was from where we ate dinner today, in Abbeville, twelve miles north of Oxford. Brother Will said he and that man from Abbeville crashed in Chattanooga and that neither one of them had any business being out of Lafayette County.

He used to go down to the coast, and he liked it. Back in the twenties and thirties, Jack Stone, Phil Stone's brother, was really a friend to him. Phil Stone was his friend more than anything else. But he did encourage him. Jack had a law office and lived in Charleston. Brother Will used to go to Charleston, and Jack Stone and his wife also had a house on the Gulf Coast in Pascagoula and used to spend summer times there. Brother Will was there many summers. So, he did like the Gulf Coast.

11. Paul Dilwyn Summers, Jr., husband of Jill Faulkner Summers.

S. Wolff: Would you explain how he named the houseboat?

J. Faulkner: The name was *Minmagary*. It was a combination of the names of the wives of the men who owned the boat. Their names were Minnie Ruth Little, wife of Dr. Ashford Little; Maggie Brown, Ross Brown's wife; and Colonel Evans' wife.[12] I can't think of what her name is now. Colonel Evans was a friend of Brother Will's when he built the boat in the 1950s.[13] He used to teach at Ole Miss. After he retired, he stayed in Oxford.

S. Wolff: Do you see Memphis as a city in Faulkner's fiction that has negative symbolic connotations of temptation, sin, and death?

J. Faulkner: Yes. You know, he took Aunt Estelle to a whorehouse up there one time.

S. Wolff: He took his wife to one?

J. Faulkner: They were in the Peabody Hotel, and she said, "I know you've been to whorehouses, and I want to go to one." Brother Will said, "All right." He called a lady, who was Miss Reba's equivalent, and they sat around and had coffee and a few drinks.[14]

S. Wolff: Did William Faulkner feel a conflict about literally owning land?

J. Faulkner: Yes, Brother Will felt a conflict about owning land. He owned land, but didn't like to see it exploited. He didn't like anybody or anything exploited.

S. Wolff: Did your uncle have a good sense of humor?

J. Faulkner: He pulled a good one on me, once. He came back from South America—hell, I was thirty-five years old—and said, "I know where we are going hunting next." I said, "All right, where?" He said, "We are going to hunt tigers in Venezuela," and I said, "That's great."

We talked two or three weeks. We were planning this trip to hunt tigers, and he told me how to do the tiger roar, and how many tigers we were going to kill. I went and bought a rifle, a good one, and I kept

12. Mary Evans, wife of Colonel Hugh Evans (Blotner, *Faulkner: A Biography*, II, 1256).

13. For further details on the construction of the *Minmagary*, see *ibid.*, 1254–56.

14. In this section Jimmy Faulkner refers to several characters in William Faulkner's novels *Light in August*, *The Sound and the Fury*, and *Sanctuary*.

telling John, my daddy, that Brother Will and I were going tiger hunting down in Venezuela, South America, and John kept looking at me sort of funny. I kept on talking, and he said, "Are you sure?" I said, "Yes, sir."

Finally, he said, "Look, Bill's pulling your leg; there are no tigers in South America"—and that's right. I didn't know that. I was all ready to go. I believed everything he said. So I looked it up and found out there aren't any tigers down there. I went to Brother Will and said, "There aren't any tigers down there," and he said, "I know it." He teased me like that once in a while.

He may have made up for it, though, about a year later. He was drinking one night, and I went to look after him because Aunt Estelle was in Virginia. He was restless, so we went riding in the car. When we came home, he said, "Go get the deer rifle." This was the one we were going to hunt tigers with. He gave it to me.

S. Wolff: At the end of *Absalom, Absalom!* Shreve says to Quentin: "Why do you hate the South?" and Quentin says, "I don't hate it; I don't hate it." [15] Would you comment upon Faulkner's feelings about the South?

J. Faulkner: He compared himself with General Lee in a lot of ways. Not as a general, because he wasn't one, but in his devotion to his home state and his home section of the country. "I don't hate it; I don't hate it"—that sounds like he is trying to convince himself that he doesn't hate it. That's not true. Brother Will didn't hate it; he loved it. [16] We got in a pretty good discussion one time, and I told him I thought the United States should be divided into five sections because we are five different kinds of people—the South, the West, the Far West, the Middle West, and the East—but that we should have a common market like Europe has and a common defense pact. He agreed that we were a different section of the country.

S. Wolff: Was it Oxford, the place, that influenced William Faulkner's imagination?

J. Faulkner: No, it wasn't Oxford, the place. He would have done the same thing if he had been in New York. But he wouldn't have had the

---

15. Faulkner, *Absalom, Absalom!*, 378.

16. Faulkner articulated his love-hate relationship with the South in *Faulkner at Nagano*, 26, ed. Jelliffe, 126–27, as well as in his fiction.

impact of the southern town. He would have taken any place and written what he did. He heard the stories of the county told by others in the days when people sat around and talked. He would hear stories from travelers. He said he was not a historian but rather a recorder. He wrote what he saw and heard.[17]

S. Wolff: Would you say William Faulkner treated you more like a younger brother or a son?

J. Faulkner: To me he was half way between father and brother. We happened to like the same things—hunting and flying—and in World War II, I had done the things he wanted to do in World War I.

S. Wolff: How did your uncle feel about your military experience?

J. Faulkner: He liked it! I became a lieutenant colonel two years before Brother Will died. He was proud of my title because it represented a tradition. He said, "We've got another colonel in the family."[18]

S. Wolff: What did you say to William Faulkner when he received the Nobel Prize?

J. Faulkner: One day after he got the Nobel Prize—we hunted in afternoons—he was putting his boots on in the library, and I said: "Brother Will, congratulations on that prize." He said, "Fine. Let's go hunting."

S. Wolff: You were a pilot during World War II, weren't you?

J. Faulkner: Yes. Halfway between Okinawa and Japan, my plane got hit in the engine, but I was going fast enough to get back over the water, and I flew it about thirty minutes until it finally gave out, and I landed in the water. That was in the morning, and they sent a destroyer to get me; they picked me up that afternoon. It didn't really bother me. We had gone through all the training and all you go through to prepare you for when something like that happens. We were flying cover for the destroyer fleet all the time because they were being hit by kamikazes so bad.

17. See William Faulkner's own explanation: "I don't think . . . one topography will produce a writer where another topography won't" (Frederick L. Gwynn and Joseph L. Blotner, eds., *Faulkner in the University: Class Conferences at the University of Virginia, 1957–58* [Charlottesville, 1959], 138).

18. See Blotner, *Faulkner: A Biography,* II, 1831.

A destroyer picked me up, and the destroyer captain sent me over to the hospital ship before dark. They gave me a physical, and then they sent me back to the air strip the next morning, and I started flying again that day.[19]

S. Wolff: That's a good war story. Do you have a plate in your head, too?

J. Faulkner: No, but I have a scar on my cheek from the crash!

S. Wolff: Did Estelle Faulkner give many interviews?

J. Faulkner: No interviews that I know of. Jill also gave very few. Joe Blotner, of course, did the biography following Brother Will's death. In Stockholm, when he was there for the Nobel Prize, someone said that Blotner should talk to Brother Will's butler; it was the butler's duty to go through Brother Will's trash and find unopened invitations. The butler gave Blotner the first draft for the Nobel Prize speech—he got it out of his trash. Jill has not wanted to give many interviews. She says, "I've stayed away and kept my boys away from the hype, but I want them to have something." She stays away from it. So this is the first interview of this length that I know of.

S. Wolff: Would you tell us about your uncle's last days?

J. Faulkner: About the middle of June in 1962, Brother Will had just gotten these two new horses: an iron gray named Stonewall and a black named Beauregard. They were from Oklahoma, and they were fractious horses. Stonewall was the worse of the two, and that's the one he liked to ride. He was riding one afternoon about the middle of June just as they were getting ready to build the by-pass. He would ride down there into the woods.[20]

By the middle of the afternoon, the horse came back by itself, and Aunt Estelle started to get people ready to look for him when he walked into the driveway holding his back. He walked straight to the barn where the horse went and got on the horse to show it that it couldn't better him. I went down the next day, and he was holding his back. I just

19. See *ibid.*, 1201, for further details.
20. See Blotner, *Faulkner: A Biography*, II, 1827–46, for further details on Faulkner's last days. See also, Marshall, "Scenes from Yoknapatawpha," 263–67.

had a wisdom tooth cut out, and Dr. Burgoyne had given me a bottle of Demerol pills, and I was scared to take them. After a couple of days, I said, "I've got something that will cut the pain out of your back." He said, "I will not take it; I will not take even aspirin. I might get addicted to it." I said, "You're crazy as hell if you're hurting, and you don't have to." This went on for a couple of weeks.

About the second or third of July, I guess it was, he had just had it and started to drink. He didn't want to drink that much at that time. He planned his drinking times. Well, I was down there on the third, and he might have had a half of a fifth of gin. He was on that bed in the office, in that little single bed downstairs. The next day, I believe, he started the second bottle, which was very little for him, and he said he wanted to go to Byhalia. That's where the sanitorium, the drying-out hospital, was. On the fourth I said, "All right, I'll come down this afternoon, and we will go." So I went down, and it was hot, golly. I said, "Brother Will, it's pretty hot. Would you like to go this afternoon or maybe wait until to-morrow until it's cooler?" He said, "Well, tomorrow."

I went down there the next morning, and he was sort of restless, but not ready. I said, "You really want to go?" He said, "Let's wait." I returned that afternoon, and he said, "I'm ready to go." So we got into the car and went to Byhalia. I checked him in about 6:00 P.M.—maybe, late afternoon. It was an old home. Brother Will's room was pretty big— a little bit bigger than this one. It had two double beds in it, and it was right next to the nurses' station. There was a doctor, an M.D. who owned the hospital, who checked his blood pressure and all that stuff, and I stayed there till about 10:00 P.M.

Brother Will always knew exactly what was going on—his mind was clear, so I could understand what he was saying because I had been around him enough when he was like that to know what his words were.

The room had two double beds in it, one across the room from the other. Brother Will was in one bed, and I sat on the other bed for a while and talked to him. About 10:00 or 10:30 P.M., I decided to come home. I really don't think he knew I was in the room at that time because I was sitting on the other bed while they were working with him. I crossed the room and went over to his bed. I walked up to him on the left side of the bed and took his left hand in my left hand. I said, "Brother Will." When he heard my voice, his eyes cleared up, and his voice did, too. I said, "When you get ready to come home, call me, and I'll come get you." He said, "Yes, Jim, I will."

I left, and I got home about midnight, I suppose, and went to sleep. At 1:30 A.M. the phone rang. Nan, my wife, picked it up. I was told that Brother Will had just died. "He had a heart attack," they later said to me. Before he died, he sat up on the side of the bed; the nurse gave him a shot to quiet him down; he groaned and lay back down; and then he died. Brother Will had never had any sign of heart trouble.

When Nan put the phone down, I knew Aunt Estelle was down at Rowan Oak by herself, so, as soon as I called John, my daddy, I dressed and went to Rowan Oak as quick as I could. Aunt Estelle, naturally, was shaken up. She was not a strong woman physically, so I called Chester McLarty, our doctor. He came down and stayed with us until well after daylight.

I called the ambulance here in Oxford and asked them to go to the hospital in Byhalia to get Brother Will's body. I called the hospital, and they said, "We've already sent him home." The funeral home was at that time on the northeast corner of the square, and John stayed there until they brought him home.

Anyway, I got his clothes together and went up there. When Nanny died in October of 1960, not two years before he did, Brother Will and I went in and picked out her coffin. He said she wanted the cheapest way to get back to the ground. She said, "I'll be better off, and everyone else will."

He died at 1:30 A.M. that morning, and we had the funeral the next afternoon. Everybody was here in Oxford. When we picked out Nanny's coffin, it was a small one, and Brother Will said, "That's exactly what I want." So when I took the clothes up to the funeral home, I picked out the coffin exactly like hers.

When they brought him home about 6:00 that morning, I believe, they put him in the living room in front of the fireplace. I went upstairs to see Aunt Estelle about something; I forget what it was. Anyway, it took a little while. When I came back, he was gone! John was there, and I said, "What in the hell happened?" He said, "So and so thought he should have a better coffin, so they sent him back to the funeral home to get another coffin." I said, "I'll be damned." John said, "Leave it alone. Bill's up there laughing like hell right now with the trouble he's causing, even now." It really was funny after it was over. I said, "All right."

They brought back this atrocious damn thing. It was to be a closed casket. In the old South, when the servants wanted to see the body, they did. So they asked me if they could open the casket and show him. I said, "Yes, I'm sure it will be all right." So I asked Jill and Estelle, and they said, "Sure." So everybody got out of the room, and the servants went in. They were the last ones who saw him—the only ones who saw him, I think.

People came from everywhere. The reporters were real understanding, in a way. John had asked the guard on the gate to keep people out, including reporters. We realized the reporters had a job to do, so Jack and I met them in the back room of a restaurant here in town—it's burned now. We had a question-and-answer game, and they wanted to know if they could take a picture of him in the coffin. I said, "No."

Jack was a real firm person. He had a Jekyll-and-Hyde personality. He was the epitome of a southern gentleman, but he was also FBI. He laid the ground rules. Paul Flowers[21] happened to be down here at the time, so he called me and came out to my house. I asked him if he would be the spokesman for the newspeople, and he said, "If they will let me." I said, "We will just tell them that's the only way we will go along with it." So he did, and they were really pretty nice to us. That's the way it happened.

S. Wolff: When did you realize the scope of your uncle's achievements?

J. Faulkner: One day I simply realized that Brother Will's works would go down in history.

21. Paul Abbott Flowers, educator and journalist, taught at several universities, including Memphis State University, and served as book editor and columnist for the Memphis *Commercial Appeal.*

APPENDIX A

History of the *U* in *Faulkner*

J. Faulkner: About the mid-1950s I used to go by and talk to Uncle John. Uncle John was J. T. Falkner II, my granddaddy's younger brother. He was a lawyer in Oxford and a good storyteller, and he told me about our name. He said that years and years ago it was spelled *Falconer* because the people we come from were falconers in the king's court. Then he told me that somewhere a German got involved in the family and that there was a Baron von Falconer. Well, he said, our family had to leave England and went to France and stayed for a generation. That's probably where one wandered over into Germany and got the Baron von Falconer. I don't know.

But as they got tired of France, two brothers came to America. They landed in Charleston, South Carolina, and at that time they were spelling the name *Faulkner*. One of the brothers stayed in South Carolina around Charleston. The other one went to North Carolina around Hayward County. Uncle John told me that during the Revolutionary War, there was a Sergeant Faulkner at the Battle of Cowpens. Because of his activities and his participation in the war, he was granted some land by the government.

One of the brothers, Joseph, left and married Caroline Word, of Georgia. The name still was spelled *Faulkner.* He and Caroline Word married and had a child—James. They wanted to go to Missouri and set out in a wagon. They got as far as Knoxville. Another baby was going to be born, so they had to stay there for a year.

This baby was the man we called the Old Colonel, William C. Faulkner, my great-great-granddaddy. Well, after he was a year old, they went on to St. Genevieve, Missouri. They stayed there until William or Bill—whatever they called the Old Colonel—was about fourteen years old. This was around 1838. He was born in 1825.

He and his brother were in the cornfield chopping corn and they got in a fight. William hit his brother with a hoe—thought he killed him and he ran. His mother had a brother, Thomas Word—a lawyer in Pontotoc, Mississippi, which was about fifteen or twenty miles south of Ripley. Well, this fourteen-year-old boy walked for three months and finally made it to Pontotoc. When he got to Pontotoc, he found out that Thomas Word was away on business. He sat down on the street and started crying, and this little girl stopped to talk to him and took him home with her. They fed him, and he told her when he got cleaned up that he was going to Ripley. His mother had a sister, Justiania Word, who had married John Wesley Thompson, and was living in Ripley. So he started to Ripley, but he told this girl that one day he was going to come back and marry her. Eventually, he did, I can't think of her name—the Old Colonel's second wife [Lizzie H. Vance]. But, anyway, when he got to Ripley, he found his aunt's husband, who was John Wesley Thompson, in jail for murder. John Wesley Thompson studied law while he was in jail and defended himself. He was later appointed district attorney. That is where the Old Colonel studied law—in his office. Well, his name was still spelled *Faulkner,* and later on, a few years later, a family moved to Tippah County, where Ripley is, and they also spelled their name *Faulkner.* He didn't like them. He didn't want to be connected to them, so he dropped the *u.*

S. Wolff: The Old Colonel?

J. Faulkner: The Old Colonel dropped the *u.* Somewhere I have a bit of stationery with it spelled both ways on it. Anyway, the *u* stayed out of the name until 1919, 1920, 1921. Brother Will put the *u* back in his name. The story is around that an agent inadvertently put the *u* in his name, but that is not true because he had the *u* in his name before he wrote his first book.

So, anyway, he was the only one who had the *u* in his name until about 1939, when my daddy, John Falkner, wrote his first book, *Men Working.* He sent it to New York to an agent, and the agent asked him if he minded if they put the *u* in his name. That would make it sell better. John wrote back and said, "I don't give a damn what you do—sell it." So they put the *u* back in my daddy's name.

My younger brother put the *u* back in his name because my daddy did. I didn't, at first, because I was getting ready to go into the Marine Corps and on my birth certificate my name is spelled without the *u*. So I spelled my last name without the *u* until I got out of the Marine Corps in 1946.

When I came home I asked John, my daddy, if he was going to keep the *u* in his name, and he said, "Yes, I am." Well, I said, "If you do, because of you, I will, too." So I put the *u* in my name, too. So, because I did, my younger brother took it out of his name. So it's spelled both ways—however you want to spell it. That's as near as I can remember [laughter].

I ran into a descendant of the brother that stayed in Charleston, South Carolina, in Pensacola in 1943. His name is Smokey Faulkner, and he still spelled his name with the *u*. We figured out that we were distant cousins, that our great-great-great-great-granddaddies were brothers. That's it.

APPENDIX B

Maps of Lafayette County and Yoknapatawpha County

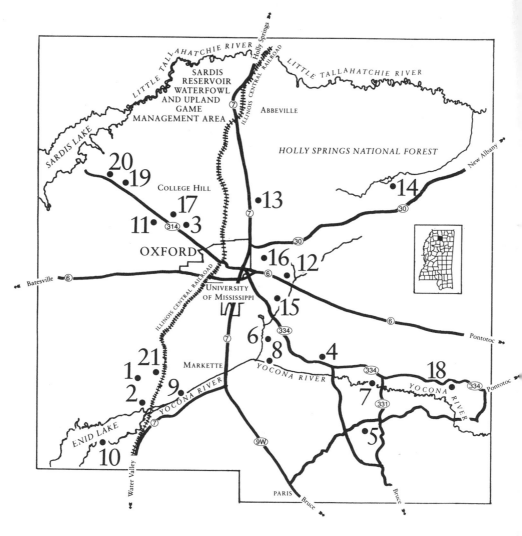

Map of Lafayette County, Mississippi, showing some of the
locations visited during the interviews.

KEY

1. THE OLD JONES PLACE
2. THE SHIPP HOME
3. JIMMY FAULKNER'S HOUSE
4. YOCONA (THE TOWN)
5. TULA
6. GRANDMA HARKINS' FARM
7. NEAR TULA (PRICE CROSSING OVER THE YOCONA RIVER)
8. FUDGETOWN (CANTRELL CROSSING OVER THE YOCONA RIVER)
9. TAYLOR CROSSING (CONCRETE BRIDGE OVER THE YOCONA RIVER)
10. BRIGHAM YOUNG (PROSPECT CROSSING OVER THE YOCONA RIVER)
11. COLLEGE HILL CHURCH
12. DOGTROT HOUSE
13. DEAD MAN'S CURVE
14. WILLIAM FAULKNER'S FARM (JOE PARKS'S FARM)
15. YELLOWLEAF CREEK
16. RIVERS HILL
17. MISS PEARLE'S STORE
18. MOTEE'S JUKE JOINT
19. TOBY TUBBY CEMETERY
20. WASH JONES'S CABIN MIGHT HAVE BEEN LOCATED IN AN AREA LIKE THIS
21. TAYLOR

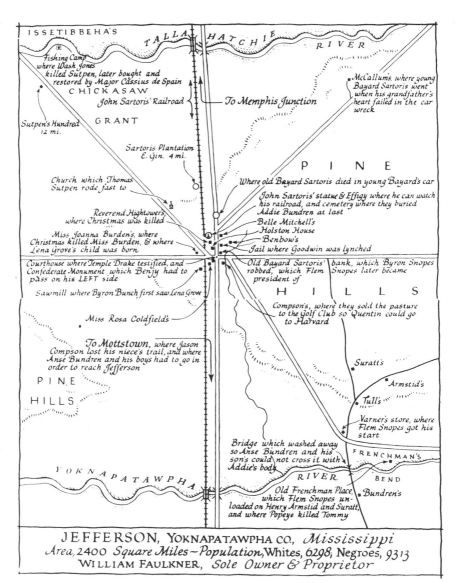

Faulkner's map of Yoknapatawpha County. *From Absalom, Absalom! by William Faulkner. Copyright © 1936 by William Faulkner and renewed 1964 by Estelle Faulkner and Jill Faulkner Summers. Reprinted by permission of Random House, Inc.*

BIBLIOGRAPHY

SELECTED WORKS BY WILLIAM FAULKNER

Absalom, Absalom! New York, 1936.
As I Lay Dying. New York, 1930.
Collected Stories of William Faulkner. New York, 1950.
A Fable. New York, 1954.
"Go Down, Moses" and Other Stories. New York, 1942.
The Hamlet. New York, 1940.
Intruder in the Dust. New York, 1948.
Light in August. New York, 1932.
The Mansion. New York, 1959.
Requiem for a Nun. New York, 1951.
Sanctuary. New York, 1931.
The Sound and the Fury. New York, 1929.
The Town. New York, 1951.
The Unvanquished. New York, 1934.

LETTERS

Blotner, Joseph, ed. *Selected Letters of William Faulkner.* New York, 1978.
Cowley, Malcolm, ed. *The Faulkner-Cowley File: Letters and Memories, 1944–62.* New York, 1966.
Letters to Sally Wolff from:
  Bahr, Howard. September 12, 1991.
  McGuire, Carolyn R. August 10, 1993.

PUBLISHED INTERVIEWS

Gwynn, Frederick L., and Joseph L. Blotner, eds. *Faulkner in the University: Class Conferences at the University of Virginia, 1957–58.* Charlottesville, 1959.

Jelliffe, Robert A. *Faulkner at Nagano*. Toyko, 1956.

Meriwether, James B., and Michael Millgate, eds. *Lion in the Garden: Interviews with William Faulkner, 1926–62*. New York, 1968.

BIOGRAPHICAL WORKS ABOUT FAULKNER AND HIS FAMILY

Blotner, Joseph. *Faulkner: A Biography*. 2 vols. New York, 1974.

Brodsky, Louis Daniel. *William Faulkner: Life Glimpses*. Austin, 1990.

Duclos, Donald Philip. "Son of Sorrow: The Life, Works and Influence of Colonel William C. Falkner, 1825–1889." Ph.D. dissertation, University of Michigan, 1962.

Falkner, Murry C. *The Falkners of Mississippi: A Memoir*. Baton Rouge, 1967.

Faulkner, Jim. *Across the Creek: Faulkner Family Stories*. Jackson, Miss., 1986.

―――. "Brother Will's Passing." *Southern Living* (March, 1992), 108–109.

Faulkner, John. *my brother Bill: An Affectionate Reminiscence*. New York, 1963.

Minter, David. *William Faulkner: His Life and Work*. Baltimore, 1982.

Webb, James W., and A. Wigfall Green, eds. *William Faulkner of Oxford*. Baton Rouge, 1965.

CRITICAL AND HISTORICAL STUDIES

Bahr, Howard L. "Faulkner's Military Aviators." M.A. thesis, University of Mississippi, 1980.

Bassett, John Earl. *William Faulkner: An Annotated Checklist of Criticism*. New York, 1972.

Brown, Calvin S. *A Glossary of Faulkner's South*. New Haven, Conn., 1976.

Coleman, Mark T. *Politics and Punishment: The History of the Louisiana State Penal System*. Baton Rouge, 1971.

Coughlan, Robert. *The Private World of William Faulkner*. New York, 1954.

Cullen, John B., with Floyd C. Watkins. *Old Times in the Faulkner Country*. Baton Rouge, 1975.

Curran, Charles Howard, and Carl Kauffeld. *Snakes and Their Ways*. New York, 1937.

Dain, Martin J. *Faulkner's County: Yoknapatawpha*. New York, 1964.

Ditmars, Raymond Lee. *A Field Book of North American Snakes*. Garden City, N.Y., 1948.

―――. *The Reptiles of North America: A Review of the Crocodilians, Lizards, Snakes, Turtles and Tortoise Inhabiting the United States and Northern Mexico*. New York, 1936.

East Tennessee Historical Society Magazine, XXX (1958), 98; XXXI (1959), 69.

Faust, Patricia L., ed. *Historical Times Illustrated Encyclopedia of the Civil War.* New York, 1986.

"Federal Surplus Relief Corporation." *United States Government Organization Manual.* Washington, D.C., 1942.

Ford, Margaret Patricia, and Suzanne Kincaid. *Who's Who in Faulkner.* Baton Rouge, 1963.

Hathorn, John Cooper. *Early Settlers of Lafayette Co., Mississippi: A Period of Study of Lafayette County from 1836–1860, with Emphasis on Population Groups.* Oxford, Miss., 1980.

Howell, Elmo. "William Faulkner's Graveyard." *Notes on Mississippi Writers,* IV (1972), 115–18.

Kerr, Elizabeth. *Yoknapatawpha: Faulkner's "Little Postage Stamp of Native Soil."* New York, 1976.

Kirk, Robert W., with Marvin Klotz. *Faulkner's People: A Complete Guide and Index to Characters in the Fiction of William Faulkner.* Berkeley, 1963.

Kirwan, Albert Dennis. *Revolt of the Rednecks: Mississippi Politics, 1876–1925.* Gloucester, Mass., 1964.

Lafayette County Courthouse. *Sectional Index to Lands in Lafayette County, Mississippi. Sections 1–36, Township 9-South, Range 4-West.* XXII. Oxford, Miss., n.d.

Langford, Beverly Young. "History and Legend in William Faulkner's 'Red Leaves.'" *Notes on Mississippi Writers,* VI (1972), 21–22.

Lawrence, John, and Dan Hise. *Faulkner's Rowan Oak.* Jackson, Miss., 1993.

Loewen, James W., and Charles Sallis, eds. *Mississippi: Conflict and Change.* New York, 1974.

McHaney, Thomas L. "The Falkners and the Origin of Yoknapatawpha County: Some Corrections." *Mississippi Quarterly: A Journal of Southern Culture* XXV (Summer, 1972), 249–64.

———. *William Faulkner: A Reference Guide.* Boston, 1976.

Marshall, Emma Jo Grimes. "Scenes from Yoknapatawpha: A Study of People and Places in the Real and Imaginary Worlds of William Faulkner." Ph.D. dissertation, University of Alabama, 1978.

Meriwether, James B. "Faulkner's Mississippi." *Mississippi Quarterly: A Journal of Southern Culture,* XXV (Spring, 1972), 15–24.

———. "William Faulkner." In *Fifteen Modern American Authors,* edited by Jackson R. Bryer. Durham, N.C., 1969.

Miner, Ward L. *The World of William Faulkner.* New York, 1959.

Mississippi State Department of Public Welfare. *Third Biennial Report, July 1, 1939–June 3, 1941.* Jackson, Miss., 1941.

Pate, Frances Willard. "Names of Characters in Faulkner's Mississippi." Ph.D. dissertation, Emory University, 1969.

Pilkington, John. *Stark Young.* Boston, 1985.

Polk, Noel. "The Critics and Faulkner's 'Little Postage Stamp of Native Soil.'" *Mississippi Quarterly: A Journal of Southern Culture,* XXIII (Summer, 1970), 323–35.

Price-Stephens, Gordon. "Faulkner and the Royal Air Force." *Mississippi Quarterly: A Journal of Southern Culture,* XVII (Summer, 1964), 123–28.

Roller, David C., and Robert W. Twyman, eds. *The Encyclopedia of Southern History.* Baton Rouge, 1979.

Rosenbloom, Morris Victor. *The Liquor Industry: A Survey of Its History, Manufacture, Problems of Control and Importance.* Braddock, Pa., 1936.

Skipwith Historical and Genealogical Society. *The Heritage of Lafayette County, Mississippi.* Oxford, Miss., 1986.

———. *Lafayette County, Mississippi, Cemetery Records.* Oxford, Miss., 1978.

Smith, G. E. Kidder, ed. *The Architecture of the United States.* Garden City, N.Y., 1981.

Sobotka, C. John, Jr. *A History of Lafayette County, Mississippi.* Oxford, Miss, 1976.

Taylor, Herman E. *Faulkner's Oxford: Recollections and Reflections.* Nashville, 1990.

United States Works Progress Administration. *Mississippi: A Guide to the Magnolia State.* New York, 1949.

Waggoner, Hyatt H. *William Faulkner: From Jefferson to the World.* Lexington, Ky., 1959.

Watkins, Floyd C. "The Gentle Reader and Mr. Faulkner's Morals." *Georgia Review,* XIII (Spring, 1959), 68–75.

———. *In Time and Place.* Athens, Ga., 1977.

———. "Sacrificial Rituals and Anguish in the Victim's Heart in 'Red Leaves.'" *Studies in Short Fiction,* XXX (Winter, 1993), 71–78.

———. "William Faulkner in His Own Country." *Emory University Quarterly,* XV (1989), 228–39.

Wigginton, Eliot, ed. *The Foxfire Book: Hogdressing, Log Cabin Building, Mountain Crafts and Foods, Planting by the Signs, Snake Lore, Hunting Tales, Faith Healing, Moonshining, and Other Affairs of Plain Living.* Garden City, N.Y., 1972.

Wilson, Charles Reagan, and William Ferris, eds. *Encyclopedia of Southern Culture.* Chapel Hill, 1989.

INDEX